FIRE
IN THE DARK
MEN AND GODS

JACK DONOVAN

[DH]

DISSONANT HUM

UTAH

For current contact information, visit jack-donovan.com.

First edition published in 2020 by Jack Donovan and Brutal Company LLC, under the Dissonant Hum imprint.

At the time of publication, Brutal Company LLC was located in Salt Lake City, Utah.

FIRST EDITION

Hardcover ISBN
978-0-9854523-9-1

Paperback ISBN
978-0-9854523-8-4

Library of Congress Control Number: 2020925045

CONTENTS

Preface 13

FIRE IN THE DARK

On the Death of Gods and the Murder of Heroes ... 25
The Hliðskjálf Dilemma 33
Chaos 45
Fire in the Dark 49
Cosmos 55
Create - Champion - Perpetuate 69

PANTHEON

The Father 91
    The Father in Darkness and Light 97
    The Father as Ascended Striker 109
    Symbols of the Guardians 113
The Striker 125
    The Striker in Darkness and Light 141
The Lord of the Earth 153
    The Lord's Symbols 173
Washington 181

SOLAR IDEALISM

Solar Idealism 193

Afterword.. 203

Acknowledgements... 209

Endnotes 213

EXTRAS

Mythic Timelines 225

Bibliography and Further Reading 227

A Sky Without Goddesses 235

Stay Solar 245

PREFACE

I've written in the past about a "sky without eagles," and it's an image that's stayed with me — a sense of emptiness that searches the sky above for something worthy, something excellent, something noble, something better. As I look back over more than a decade of writing about men and masculinity, it's become clear to me that the theme of my work hasn't changed. I've been writing about the same problems with increasing levels of understanding, articulation, and refinement.

What is ideal in man? What is better? What is best? What is perfect and unreachable and, therefore...divine?

That gray sky, that polluted overhead abyss that reaches out lazily and horizontally toward some misty, indeterminable terminus — this is sadness, horror, and despair. This is chaos and the doom of the Last Man. This is the desolation that remains when the eagles have been culled to save the rabbits, the void that is left after the death of all gods and the murder of heroes. We wander through this no man's land surrounded by lost boys whose fathers were weak or absent entirely. And while it is a tragedy that boys come of age without men to look up to, perhaps it is an even greater tragedy that they have nothing beyond men that fills them with wonder — no vision of perfection. Without that light and clarity that inspires aspiration, men are left with only ressentiment and acceptance and grim resignation.

Man, for all these years... I've been trying to inspire men to do better and reach higher and somehow… with these many and desperate invocations… I've been trying to call the eagles back into the sky.

Some groups talk about the "sacred masculine," but they seem to offer little more than collective catharsis and self-affirmation — a hairier sewing circle for men who are looking for shoulders to cry on. For something to be sacred, it must be holy and consecrated, set aside, and inviolable. It must be fixed. That which is sacred should be your *axis mundi* and the anchor of your identity, and at least in theory, it should connect you to something eternal— something bigger and beyond yourself. For something to be called the "sacred masculine," it should be both legitimately sacred and legitimately masculine.

This book represents my attempt to sketch out a framework of the "sacred masculine" that is grounded in a timeless understanding of what it means to be a man, building out from the theory of masculinity outlined in my book *The Way of Men*. That book is foundational, and you may get lost or flustered if you've never read it — so start there or at least have it handy.

My exploration of the "sacred masculine" began in earnest while I was performing Germanic pagan rituals and constructing a sacred space for men in Eastern Washington known as Waldgang. Men from all over the world were interested in learning more about these rituals and my perspectives on Germanic paganism, so this book started as a response to that — originally titled "Odin, Thor, Frey." However, as my research expanded, I realized that the concepts I was talking about transcended the limitations of that frame. Germanic paganism is but one beautiful, thought-provoking, and inspiring manifestation of something much bigger and much older.

When I wrote *The Way of Men*, I referenced everything from *The Epic of Gilgamesh* to the story of Rome, and it connected with men all over the world, from every background. This book explains aspects of the "sacred masculine" using the primitive, universal metaphor of the campfire and builds on the concept of The Perimeter from *The Way of Men*.

I've been repeating the slogan "stay solar" for the past few years, and it seems to have caught on and even taken on a life of its own. I sketched out an essay explaining what I meant by it, and in the fall of 2019, I gave a speech at the 21 Convention titled "Manly Idealism" that introduced many of the ideas that I developed in this project. The original "Stay Solar" essay is included in the back of this book, for posterity.

Fire in the Dark combines the concept of solarity with "manly idealism" to produce what I'll call either a philosophical movement or a spiritual movement for men that I've named "solar idealism." I say "either" and "or" because there are two ways to read this book.

Many of my readers are Christians of various kinds, devout or otherwise, including many men who I respect, admire, and whom I consider allies and friends. I have come in contact with men who follow my work who subscribe to some form of Islam or Hinduism, and of course, there are many Germanic pagans and other kinds of neopagans. We know a large amount of what we know about the spirituality of the Ancient world because Christians found the stories of non-Christians interesting and valuable and they wrote them down. We can even thank a Muslim traveler, Ahmad ibn Fadlan, for one of the rare first-hand accounts we have of a "Viking" ritual.

If you've already committed to a spiritual discipline — or if you're an atheist who is only interested in masculine psychology — I believe that this book has a lot to offer in terms of its observations about men and myth and archetypes. If that's the case, read this book as one would read the work of Joseph Campbell or a book like *King, Warrior, Magician, Lover.*

If, however, you are not an avowed Christian or Muslim or a hardline atheist, and you are open to (or perhaps even looking for) some spiritual perspective that aligns with your masculine values but which also connects you to something bigger than and beyond yourself...I propose Solar Idealism as an alternative spiritual technology to explore.

There is an overlap between psychology and spirituality that blurs the line which separates them to the extent that any differentiation seems like little more than a preference for a particular narrative or aesthetic. In this twilight space between the plausible theory and the dream, between that which we insist is entirely conscious and that which we suspect to be unconscious, there is room for a practice of a Solar Idealism that is supra-intellectual, metaphysical, and open to mystery. In this book, I have given names to integrated concepts or forms or forces of nature that have had many names but which were likely part of the masculine experience before men spoke any language that we would recognize. I did not and could not invent the idea of a father in the sky, or a thundering warrior ideal, or a fertility god who perpetuates life and makes it joyful.

A graveyard of gods spreads out before us as we sit on our high seats and look out over the sands of time, littered with the half-sunk and crumbling visages of every Odin and Ozymandias. Yet, if we inspect the remains carefully, we can recognize some familiar aspect of ourselves in each artifact. Or, perhaps in ourselves, we can find something ancient and inherited from the great men of the past and their gods. Are the old gods projections of perfected man, or are the best portions of men the remnants or the seeds of the divine?

If we can begin with this question and leave the answer open, we can confront the challenge of this age of annihilation and begin to see eagles in our skies once more.

Throughout this book, I often refer to Proto-Indo-European language, myth, and culture. Several hundred years ago, men who studied certain languages started to notice that several of them seemed to share common roots and patterns and theorized that these languages developed from a common source. Everyone knew that English was, for the most part, a combination of Germanic languages and French, and that French and Spanish and Italian developed from Latin. But there were also similarities between Ancient Latin and Ancient Greek, the Germanic tongues, and languages spoken in India and Iran. Scholars started to wonder what the common source was between something like Ancient Sanskrit and Ancient Greek. Through debate and competing theories over the years, a theoretical root language was created following rules that predict how languages change over time. That language was called Proto-Indo-European because it is believed to have preceded all known Indo-European languages. There is no written record of this language, but the language's basic framework and vocabulary are fairly well established in the academic world. However, the spellings of words and the usage of diacritics varies so much between Wiktionary, Mallory, Puhvel, Quiles, the American Heritage Dictionary of Indo-European Roots, and other sources that I have not attempted to standardize them here.

Over time, similarities were found not only in these various languages but in the religions and cultures associated with them. Theories were developed about root myths and root cultures and in some cases, an original homeland — sometimes called the "urheimat" of the "Proto-Indo-Europeans," which is currently believed to have been in the Pontic-Caspian Steppe (now modern Ukraine). During the 19th and early 20th century, all of this speculation was massaged into a theory about an "Aryan" master race of magical caucasian conquerors. We have access to a lot more information now, and while we will probably never know exactly how the languages, myths, and cultures developed — the truth is probably a lot more complicated. The word "Aryan" probably didn't refer to what we would now call a "race" at all. It was likely a religious, cultural, and linguistic designation used among the Indo-Iranians. There is a theorized Indo-European root for the word, *h$_2$er(y)ós, but if some group of people used some version of that word in their spoken (but ultimately never written or completely lost) language, no one is entirely sure what they looked like. Genetic evidence suggests they were probably tall, brown-eyed, and had light but not "white" skin.

If you find the concepts of Proto-Indo-European language or myth interesting, read the current research on the topic, perhaps starting with *The Horse, the Wheel, and Language*, by David W. Anthony. Some more sources are listed in the bibliography at the end of this book.

There are all kinds of esoteric theories that were made up about the Aryans by various occultists in the late 19th and early 20th centuries. While some are very interesting and can even be inspiring, for the most part, they were fantasies dreamt up by kooky German parlor magicians based on limited information. However, these theories persist and are accepted too readily by people who *want* to believe them. I once had someone tell me that the word "aryan" meant "people of the sun." There is a fringe mythology that still holds onto the idea that white people are some kind of "solar race." None of this is accurate, but I wanted to address it upfront to circumvent any confusion when I talk about the Proto-Indo-Europeans or the sun or being "solar."

The Egyptians were pretty damn "solar." So were the Mesopotamians and the Aztecs. The sun has been a powerful symbol to people all around the world because it is something that all of us have always been able to see above us. The sun brought the day out of night and rendered the chaotic world of darkness intelligible across the globe long before homo sapiens evolved from his predecessors. The sun has been important to all men, everywhere, since the beginning of human time. And, like fire and light and violence, the sun is something that all men understand and something we all have in common.

Hierarchies of value and symbols of masculine virtue are being methodically and purposefully destroyed all around a world that is plunging into darkness and disorder right now. The threats to the survival of any manly idealism and even individual sovereignty itself — the threats to freedom — are so significant and pressing that any man who wants to waste hours and energy playing "whose ancestors were better?" is a fool who serious men no longer have time to entertain.

Before we begin, I want to thank you for reading this book. It has been my privilege and my humbling honor over the past few years to have been credited with inspiring a lot of men to become better versions of what they are. I hope that *Fire in the Dark* offers some clarity, some kindling, and perhaps even a spark.

I believe that the ideas in this book are ancient in origin, but perennial and eternally relevant. No man can live in the past. All we ever have is now. This is *our* time, and we will face our own challenges. How we respond to those challenges will be *our* legacy.

Stay Solar —

Jack Donovan
December 2020
Salt Lake City

"To honor both gods and men for their areté is a primitive instinct."

— Werner Jaeger, *Paideia : The Ideals of Greek Culture*

FIRE IN THE DARK

"God is dead! God remains dead! And we have killed him! How shall we console ourselves, the most murderous of all murderers? The holiest and the mightiest that the world has hitherto possessed, has bled to death under our knives — who will wipe the blood from us? With what water could we clean ourselves? What festivals, what sacred games shall we have to devise? Is not the magnitude of this deed too great for us? Shall we not ourselves have to become Gods, merely to seem worthy of it?"

—Nietzsche. *The Gay Science*

ON THE DEATH OF GODS AND THE MURDER OF HEROES

1

Nietzsche shouted that God was dead, and the whole world heard him.

The Zoroaster of Sils Maria is often mischaracterized as having attempted to kill god with his proclamations, but his statements were diagnostic. What he recognized in the world around him was a collapse of consensus about the religious narrative and, as a result, the disintegration of collective social values.

Nietzsche saw this mass disorientation as a great opportunity for a post-Christian revaluing of values — and it is. "Disappointment opens up a vista of chaos."[1] In chaos there is both space and kindling for creation. He imagined that in this vacuum of divinity and direction, a new man, unbound by ancient orthodoxies — a man beyond man — could then create his own life-affirming values.

However, the collapse of religious consensus was never resolved or replaced by another consistent consensus. The outcome of disillusionment has not been a deep soul-searching, but a dynamic moral marketplace in which "trending" moralities are driven almost entirely by the madness of crowds and a culture of complaint.

Pious Christianity fell out of fashion among elites and influencers, but ressentiment remained in the masses, who replaced the divine promise of comeuppance and communion with a utopian vision that promised an equality of outcomes and esteem in the here-and-now — or at least in that unlikely moment when perfect equality is achieved.

Nietzsche's diagnosis of deicide mutated into a malignant iconoclasm, not in the name of strength and life-affirming values as he had hoped, but in a "Harrison Bergeron"-style handicapping of all aspirational ideals.[2] The presumed absence of an afterlife or some divine authoritarian didn't result in the widespread determination of individuals to work to realize their highest potential and make the most of finite existence — it resulted in the jealous damning of talent, of natural gifts, and of inherited privilege. It produced among the proletariat an indictment of all advantage and the exaltation of the mundane and the mediocre.

This horizontal culture of leveling has been replacing the vertical culture that preceded it — a culture that looked upward for inspiration to gods in the heavens and heroes on marble pedestals. Ancient and recent heroes of men have been posthumously diabolized by the thumbs of bored and bitchy social media mobs — accused of brand spanking new sins they never knew they were committing. This has not been the destruction that precedes all creation, the upending of one order to be replaced by a new order, but the destruction of order itself — because order itself is hierarchical. Weathered bronzes have not been toppled to be replaced by fresh idols of heroic stature. The pedestals have been left empty — or have been populated with pedestrians or sympathetic figures that can never haunt passersby with greatness.

2

It is not only a god or the gods who have been murdered, but also by extension ideals and heroes — the destruction of all hierarchies. The prevailing rationale for this leveling is that by raising up an ideal form — a perfect ideal of strength, beauty, goodness, intelligence, or competence — those who are least able or willing to strive to embody that form will feel inadequate or unhappy. A reasonable desire for fair and equal treatment under the law has been perverted into an egalitarianism of all values.

As the thinking goes, men should not try to be better, because too few will be truly great, and a lot of them will stumble and fall along the way. The safer route is to stay put and learn to love oneself exactly as one is, because the struggle to be better may result in disappointment, pain, or injury. It is better not to try to reach, because one might fall. One might fail at trying to be something, so it is better not to try to be anything. One should learn to accept one's ugliness, because beauty is difficult to attain, and ultimately transient — as are all things.

The refusal to elevate an ideal of perfection because perfection is unattainable and near perfection is exceptional, is the product of a nihilistic ethos characterized by cowardice and self-loathing. And, it misses the point of idealism completely. It makes the perfect the enemy of the good. This is like saying that a man shouldn't work to become stronger because he will probably never become the strongest. That you shouldn't try to be better because you'll never be the best.

An ideal is not a destination, it is a direction. Without direction, there is only chaos and dissolution.

3

Psychologist Carl Jung is often credited, at least by many of his adherents, with a gift of prophecy. In his *Red Book*, an exploratory project that remained private until decades after his death, he recorded a vision of himself ambushing and murdering Siegfried, the archetypal Germanic hero, "through trickery and cunning."[3] After committing this cowardly crime he felt tormented by it and searched his soul for his underlying motivation. Jung concluded that, "The hero must fall for the sake of our redemption, since he is the model and demands imitation."[4]

In this allegorical riff on a Nietzschean theme, Jung seemed to suggest that men must murder their heroes, or refuse to have heroes in the first place, because heroes are the enemies of the true individual. That until we stop copying others, we will be nothing more than pale imitations.

This is another common reason that has been given for doing away with heroes and high ideals — that we are somehow inauthentic or derivative when we aim to reproduce greatness. But, as perfection is impossible, so is perfect reproduction. All of the variables will always be different. A man is only capable of being himself. No matter how hard he tries to be like another man, he will never be the same. He will always be a unique variation on a theme.

No matter how independent you think you are, you learn through imitation. We all do. It's how we learn everything from language to martial arts. Monkey see, monkey do. And then, when you have some idea what you are doing, you can innovate. That's where the art is.

To choose qualities in another man that you wish to imitate or emulate means that you are choosing qualities that you value and wish to reproduce in yourself. I haven't met a man of substantial accomplishment who never had a mentor or a model or an ideal or someone he looked up to at some point. Caesar wept in front of a statue of Alexander the Great.

They say that "imitation is the sincerest form of flattery," but the word flattery itself implies excessive or insincere praise. A better word is "honor." By imitating another man, you are acknowledging that he is better than you at something — whether it is a skill or a virtuous quality — and that you want to become better at it, or as good as he is, or possibly even better. By imitating him, you are honoring him based on his reputation or his demonstrated expertise or simply by the way he conducts himself.

Imitation is also a consequence of inspiration. Gods, heroes, and ideals inspire us. The forms and the stories point the way — they give us direction and show us what is possible or admirable. Exemplars and paradigms push us to overcome ourselves and maximize our potential.

4

I once attended a defensive handgun class taught by my friend Greg Hamilton, who is a former Green Beret. He told his students that one of the things they could do to cultivate the right mindset to handle an emergency that may require lethal force was to read stories about other people who have survived and overcome extreme situations. His point was that in times of stress, we remember powerful stories of courage and those stories inspire us to face our own challenges with courage. When you know that men have done extraordinary things, it expands your perception of what is possible and suggests the possibility of doing the extraordinary yourself.

5

Men don't need to hear stories about men who learned to love themselves "just the way they were." Those stories don't make men better. Hollow affectations of self-affirmation can only make men superficially content, because they will always know deep down they could have been better than "good enough."

Men need to hear stories about men who are the best, because it drives them to be better.

Why elevate and affirm what is merely acceptable when you can tell stories about the exemplary and imagine what is perfect?

Men need gods and heroes and ideals — not to beg and wallow before, but to inspire them to reach higher and lift themselves up in imitation of paragons, and in imitation of righteousness itself.

Men need gods and heroes and ideals because our conception of what is best — of what is the highest good — orients our entire value system and helps us to order our external and internal worlds.

If we cannot determine what is sacred to us, then everything is profane by default. I believe that many men today feel lost and are looking for some sense of what is sacred to give their lives meaning, order, and direction.

6

Myths and perfect ideals are often dismissed by so-called realists as delusional, childish stories for more primitive people. They say that they aren't "real."

A lot of good ideas in this book were influenced by Plato, but Plato hated myth. He wanted to censor poets and believed that poets told "the greatest lies about the greatest things."

However, in banishing myth from our lives, men have not banished baseness or desire —only beauty and magic. Men have sheltered themselves from all that is high and huddled in the shade to muddle with that which is low —believing perhaps that they'll be happy as pigs in shit.

Men interact with myths and ideals in the way that we interact with art and fiction. Myths and ideals (and art and fiction) excite the unconscious mind. Myths and ideals are the stuff of dreams.

Nightmares reveal our primal fears, but dreams also reveal our primal and unconscious aspirations — speaking to us in archetypes and symbols that are not confined by the constraints of our more mundane waking worlds.

Psychologically speaking, religious or spiritual practice gives us the opportunity to align our conscious world with our unconscious world. To align our spoken ideals with our dreams. And, in some sense, to impose order on the chaos of the unconscious. To dream the dreams that help us reach higher, by dreaming what is beyond our reach.

With open eyes, we leap, but in dreams —we fly.

We overcome our fears during the day, and in dreams, we slay dragons.

It seems that the Last Men and the people of ressentiment and so-called reason have abandoned the worlds of myths and dreams and ideals and left themselves with nothing but nightmares.

7

In the absence of gods and heroes and ideals, in the absence of any divine or virile hierarchy —in this post-Nietzschean desolation — men find themselves on the ground looking upward at "a sky without eagles." No unreachable exemplars soaring above.

Voltaire famously wrote that "If God did not exist, it would be necessary to invent him."

The gods and heroes of old may seem to be dead, and the sky above may seem empty, but I don't believe that it is necessary to "invent" gods.

Men have enshrined the same strength-based, life-affirming concepts and archetypes in myth for thousands of years. They've been looking up to the same gods and holding up the same fundamental ideals — they simply kept renaming them and reshaping them to make them culturally relevant and familiar.

The myriad pantheons of the ancient world all impart a timeless manly idealism, anthropomorphizing the best in men and their eternal functions. To revere these ideals is to revere the best in ourselves — to revere our own potential for excellence, our own spark of divinity.

If we were to look up again from this godless wasteland to see gods and eagles in the sky once more, how would we name them?

And what would they represent to us?

"In Asgard is a place called Hliðskjálf, and when Odin seated himself there in the high-seat, he saw over the whole world, and what every man was doing, and he knew all things that he saw..."

—"Gylfaginning," *Prose Edda.* Snorri Sturluson. (1220).
Translated by Rasmus Björn Anderson[5]

THE HLIÐSKJÁLF DILEMMA

8

After the Germanic god Odin crafted the world that we know, he and his brothers made men and women — endowing them with life and spirit and reason and all of the senses. Then he built a stronghold for himself and his own kin, and called it Asgard. Asgard means "the enclosure of the Aesir," an Old Norse name for the gods. Within the walls of this grand perimeter high above our world, a great hall was built and roofed with silver. It was known as *Valaskjálf*, or "shelf of the slain." Inside this hall, there was a place where Odin sat, named *Hliðskjálf*[6], the "mountainside shelf." From this high seat, Odin could see and understand everything in our world, though there were mysteries beyond that were unknown even to him.

9

Most of the men who lived in ages before us were far more isolated than we are today. The world that they knew for their entire lives may not have extended much farther than what they could see from the nearest hill or mountaintop. There have always been explorers and interactions between tribes, and cosmopolitan centers of cultural exchange have existed throughout written history. But the majority of men have lived in homogenous communities — and in these homogenous communities, one myth or narrative prevailed and was taught to children. Literacy was comparatively rare. Books were written and copied by hand, and few had access to them. Most men were taught one mythic system, one story about the world, and they accepted it and it became part of their tribal and personal identity. The story that they were taught about the world shaped the way that they perceived events and phenomena and human relationships. That story, or set of stories, organized their perception of the world and their place in it, guided them through the challenges of life, and helped them to process and accept that which was beyond their understanding.

A learned man wandering the Library of Alexandria had access to less information about the world and its ancient religions than any man today can pull up on his cell phone. Some details may have been lost in the fire and along the way, but we can see farther — all the way to the Orient, and to continents then undiscovered —and the scope of the history we can access spans thousands, tens of thousands, even millions of years.

The men of today can see the everything from high above, as if from those satellites in orbit that receive and transmit their words and pictures. What's more, they can see all time, or all that remains and the stories that were told about times gone by. We are like Odin, sitting at Hliðskjálf, looking out over everything and all time and all of the known peoples of the world who have ever lived. We can read all of their stories and behold — at some distance — the mythic splendor of every pantheon.

10

This position creates a dilemma.

Joseph Campbell wrote that the difference between myth and religion is that myth is simply, "other people's religion."[7]

Some men are still raised with and choose to adhere to a single religion or mythical system or story about the world. Good for them. The rest of us, whether we were raised without religion or turned away from one or just never came across anything that grabbed us enough to exclude all other possibilities and commit to one worldview — we're in the high seat. We can look out over everything and all time and see the connections between one person's religion and another. We can see how one story transformed into another story, one myth into another myth, one word to another word — *orð mér af orði orðs leitaði.*[8] We can trace the path of the Phoenician "shin" ʷ and watch it become the Ancient Greek sigma Σ, and with bemused and curious wonder, speculate as to how and when it became the Elder Futhark rune sowilo ᛋ, and then the Younger Futhark rune sol ᚼ, and also at some point the Latin letter "S," that I'm uSing to write thiS book and that you're uSing to read it. That's a four thousand year old squiggle for the same sound. (There are derivations in Arabic, Hebrew, and Cyrillic as well.) Snorri Sturluson, the Christian who wrote down most of the stories we know about Odin, mentioned offhandedly that Asgard was actually Troy. The Romans also claimed to be descended from the Trojans.

Once you've seen patterns like that, as they say, you can't "unsee" them.

And there are a lot of patterns like that, especially in the stories men have told about their gods and their heroes — so much so that one often gets the sense that he is reading the same story over and over again, with some changes made to the details. Like updated covers of a very old song.

11

A world is an age of man, and today's man can see all of the known worlds and ages. Every world superimposed at once on the cave wall of his consciousness, each obscuring and distorting the world above and below it, as well as his own.

Each curiosity adds a layer of understanding but also a layer of confusion.

In this way, perhaps the uncurious are less confused and more present in their own time. As the Shakers sing, perhaps it is, "a gift to be simple."

12

This leaves the rest of us everywhere and nowhere, in a state of chaos, seeking some kind of order — but which one? If you could choose any system, any frame, any guiding set of exemplars and principles from any age or any place, which one would you choose?

It's a rich man's problem. If you have access to everything, how do you figure out what you want?

We can adopt a system from here or there, but we live in our time, not theirs. Every system of myth is always going to be, to some extent, "other people's religion." This leads to a lot of cherry-picking or nerdy, anachronistic reenactment.

For most, it creates a religion à la carte. A cut of Buddhism with a side of Native American medicine man with some piping hot yoga. Namaste. Maybe finish it off with some Icelandic magical staves and a cup of good old fashioned "what would Jesus do?"

This is fine, but it's not great. The problem with a little of this and a little of that is that it's a little too conveniently flexible, and it's often philosophically incoherent. Sure, a lot of systems run together — that's one of the points I am making — but are you trying to be more like Buddha, or Odin, or Jesus, or Shiva...or what? Is your hero Ghandi or Herakles? Because you could find similarities between them, but there are also a lot of differences.

What direction are you going in, and what is going to help inspire you along the way, and where are you going to look when you're challenged or confused? Everywhere?

People tend to seek the path of least resistance, which isn't always the best path or the path to where they want to go. You can find a group of friends or an interpretation of a passage from some ancient, sacred text to validate just about anything you feel like doing at any time.

Without some kind of cohesive worldview, you're not centered—you're in a state of chaos, with no central axis or point of origin, no center of gravity, pointed nowhere, bouncing off or swept up in the gravity of whatever comes your way.

Some men synthesize their own system from all of this, determine their own values and they go forth and prosper. It's what Nietzsche would have wanted. Shine on, you crazy Übermenschen. But being a philosopher is at the very least a part-time job, and it (usually) doesn't pay very well.

I've been talking to a lot of men about philosophy and spirituality for a long time. Some of them were high performing men when I encountered them, and some were just figuring out that they wanted to become better at being men. Whether they were already good at being men or whether they had to put in some time and work to improve their strength, courage, and mastery to move in that direction — eventually they go looking for something bigger, something more. For lack of a better word, they are seeking a "spiritual" component to add depth and meaning to their lives. They don't want to let go of the hard-charging mindset that got them to wherever they are, or descend into a haze of New Age navel-gazing or half-hearted prostrations to peace and love. As a good friend of mine likes to say, "we're men...

we don't like to live in a world of lies." The men I meet are looking for a practical but motivating masculine spirituality. One that combines wisdom with strength and courage and, when wise or necessary, the capacity for violence.

13

From where we sit, we can see everything. We can pick any model of reality, any system, any pantheon. But which one? We belong to none of them, and all of them are in some sense our heritage. The superimposed snapshots of history we can see from our hand-held Hliðskjálfum are not worlds we can inhabit, but only worlds we can imagine. We can't live in or return to the past anymore than our ancestors could.

We are not in their time. We are in OUR TIME and this is OUR FATE — and as Nietzsche would say, we must love it. It is our fate to see all of these things and the connections between them.

To pick one story from another age of man is to put one's head in the sand. We have them all and we can use them all as raw materials to create a new story. Now is the time for synthesis — for integration and reconstitution.

To truly live in THIS AGE is to go swimming in this great flood of information and emerge wet and invigorated — to crawl up onto your inflatable high seat and play the plastic synthesizer of destiny.

14

I attended a workshop recently with a black belt from Europe, and as he walked around the room casually observing people with his Estonian frown, one of his refrains was: "attack transitional positions." People and ideas are often most vulnerable to attack when they are moving from one secure position to another. You can capitalize on a moment of uncertainty.

The rapid explosions of the industrial revolutions and medical advances in birth control and inexpensive travel and the global economy and eventually the Internet — all following the death of gods, the murder of heroes, and the collapse of homogenous ideals — have created a great chaos in masculine identity. Men from all over the world were suddenly unsure of who they were and what their purpose was and what they even believed.

Men from largely homogenous and isolated cultures from around the world intermingled and interacted in a way that they did previously only in cosmopolitain cities and trading centers. Their cultural definitions of masculinity were challenged and called into question by exchanges with men who appeared to be very different, but who were in many ways also very much the same. This has been among the causes of a widespread crisis of confidence in gods, heroes, and masculine ideals in almost every culture. Men everywhere are caught in a transitional position, a moment of uncertainty.

The opponents of masculinity, and by any historically consistent definition of what it means to be a man, men themselves — funded and promoted by hopeful whip-wielders and tyrants — have capitalized on this moment of uncertainty to create widespread gender confusion.

15

I wrote The Way of Men in part as a response to gender theorists who say that because ideals of masculinity have appeared to vary so widely — because masculinity has appeared to mean so many different things to so many different men from different cultures and races and religions — that masculinity means nothing at all. That there is no unifying theory of masculinity.

I didn't believe that was true. So I looked at ideals of masculinity and honor codes from many cultures and looked for the similarities and unifying themes. What I found was that men in successful and enduring cultures have always evaluated other men as men according to the same basic principles. They looked for and exalted qualities in each other that would have made men valuable in the small scale hunting and fighting bands in which we survived for the majority of our evolutionary history. The qualities that made us successful in small gangs of men who were tasked with defending the perimeters of their meaningful realities — their camps containing their women, their children, their parents, their friends and their cultures — were qualities that shaped our bodies and our minds.

16

I also believe that the mindset of men who were tasked with creating and maintaining order and safety and productivity within the perimeter of their influence shaped our spirituality and the mythic frames that have helped us to order our mental universes and make sense of the world around us. The specific details of these myths changed from tribe to tribe and people to people and civilization to civilization, but many of the overarching themes remained the same.

Leaders and visionaries, warriors, heroes, and hard workers. Men who built things and mastered nature to cultivate the land and provide sustenance. The men who pushed out into the dark in response to all of the things that went bump in the night. Lords and fathers and heads of households. These are manly archetypes that men have recognized as gods and celebrated in legend for thousands of years. They are the backbones of mythical systems that have guided and inspired men throughout human history.

17

Men today are in a transitional position, a twilight of all known gods and ideals. If men and masculinity are to survive spiritually, the distilled essence — the perfect universal spark — of these gods and ideals and archetypes must be tended and fanned and blown upon and fed kindling. People of ressentiment can tear down statues and profane greatness, but each of us carries that spark within us. It is left to us to keep it burning, to ensure that this light endures like the sun endures the endless night and the chaos of space. Like a fire in the dark.

18

In the following chapters, I will sketch out the distilled essence of an integrated masculine spirituality — my own rendering of this eternal flame.

I have chosen the word "integrated" intentionally. The word "integrate" comes from the Latin root "integro," which means "to renew, to restore, to make whole." It comes from an adjective which describes something which is complete, whole, intact, uninjured, sound, and healthy.

This project will be an imperfect and incomplete synthesis of masculine gods and heroes and archetypes, incorporating the myths and legends of linguistically related cultures with the intent of highlighting the similarities between them, drawing from the work of comparative mythologists and linguists. I say "imperfect" and "incomplete" because I'm going to confine this survey for the most part to examples from Indo-European myths and stories. I'm a Western man and that's the material I am comfortable with, and it would take years of study for me to do justice to surviving myths from Asia, Africa, Australia, or the Americas. However, men on every continent were tasked with creating order from chaos, and I am absolutely certain that parallel gods and heroes with similar functions can be found in cultures all over the world. Men are men everywhere. This work would be enriched by men who can find the same themes in cultures with which I am not adequately familiar. I believe that the root ideas and themes that I am going to discuss are relevant and important to men everywhere, and fundamental to a shared perspective.

19

So, from this high seat overlooking all things and all time, what do we have in common? What are the manifestations of masculine righteousness that we have always looked up to, the ideals to which we have always aspired, the stars that can guide us through the dark of night?

To find them, we'll go back to the beginning.

We will wander into primeval darkness and chaos, like the men who came before us.

And then we will start a fire, and start the world again from a single spark.

It has always been the work of men to imitate the cosmic work of gods.

*"The cosmos works
by harmony of tensions,
like the lyre and bow."*

— Heraclitus. *Fragments.*

"Darkness was hidden by darkness in the beginning; with no distinguishing sign, all this was water. The life force that was covered with emptiness, that one arose through the power of heat."

— The Rig Veda

CHAOS

From Ancient Greek χάος (kháos, "vast chasm, void")

20

Light can only be understood in the context of darkness.

To comprehend the light in man, and the light he is capable of creating, we must return to primordial chaos, to that state of emergency and uncertainty in which man became and becomes what he is.

21

Man is a product of nature — as much a part of the natural world as an alligator or a deer.

Each product of nature is potentially an agent of chaos to every other product of nature. The deer wanders serenely through the dappled light of the trees toward the water until the moment when the gator lunges forth to snatch it away from its gentle life and drag it into the murky depths for a panicked, choking death roll.

Nature may be objectively ordered in some impartial,

mathematical way, but subjectively speaking, every part of the natural world external to our self-awareness is a potential source of chaos. That which can be observed and measured and predicted seems somewhat less chaotic, and that which is mysterious seems all the more chaotic because its movements and dimensions and patterns are obscured. Though every aspect of nature surely has its own nature, its own way and order, that which is unknown to us is chaos. And even when we do understand it to some extent, as with a hurricane, as long as we are powerless to control it, it remains a force of chaos. A hurricane shatters order, blows it apart, and spreads it around. We must pick up the pieces to repair or remake order.

The alligator is a hurricane to the cosmos of the deer.

22

Chaos is often perceived as a frenzied randomness — the moment of the hurricane — but its ancient roots indicate a sense of a wide open abyss. The Greek root of chaos, χάος, means "emptiness, void, chasm or abyss," and comes from the verb χαίνω, "gape, be wide open..." It is suspected that this comes from the Proto-Indo-European root *ǵheh₂n-, cognate to Old English geanian, "to gape", which means, in modern English, "to yawn." It is as if the ancients somehow perceived the limitless horror of outer space —so empty and expansive that no one can hear you scream.

Cosmos is the classical opposite of chaos, although it is often illustrated with photos of space, which could be confusing without context. The word cosmos comes from the Ancient Greek word κόσμος, which means "order."

A photo of a galaxy illustrating "cosmos" is not showing the wide open space, but the order of stars and their orbiting bodies — order at the greatest conceivable scale.

The conflict between chaos and cosmos is the conflict between perceivable order and the absence of perceivable order.

23

If we zoom back in to human scale, we have primitive man wandering like a deer through the vastness of the natural world — some primeval forest that expands from tree to tree into some misty terminus or an expansive steppe of grasses undulating in the wind.

Is this openness not as terrifying as space?

To those of us who travel to wide open spaces from controlled spaces, in which we were raised and to which we will probably return, this openness may seem peaceful. But, without that context, without an *axis mundi* or conceptual anchor, one would be entirely adrift in and at the mercy of the unknown natural expanse. No road to find when you're tired of being lost. Like being black bagged and dropped into the middle of a desert.

Perfect chaos is total disorientation.

To make sense of the world is to put it in order. To create cosmos, to begin to order the world, one must establish a point of orientation — a reference point from which all distances can be measured.

Without some kind of reference point, there is no answer to the question, "where am I?"

There is only another question — "where in...relation to what?"

24

I'm going to tell you a short story about men building a beacon, a light, a point of orientation in the great expanse.

The sun and the stars and the planets and the milky way galaxy represent cosmos at the most-macro — at an interplanetary scale.

This is a story of cosmogony at the scale of a few men.

"Order and truth were born from heat as it blazed up."

— *The Rig Veda*

FIRE IN THE DARK

25

This is the story of The First Men. They were not the first men who ever lived. They are The First Men in this story about this particular fire. The First Men came from somewhere. They came from another fire and another story. There are many fires and many stories about fires. But they all start out more or less like this one.

26

The First Men were roaming through a field or a forest.

They traveled there from somewhere, but the place where they came from was no longer there, or they were no longer welcome in that place. The First Men were men who had nowhere to go, and nowhere to which they could return. In this story, they brought women and children with them, but this is not true in every story.

The First Men wandered through the vast unknown with no particular place to go. They walked through the day when the Sun was high above, illuminating all of the plants and animals and the features of the terrain as it opened up before them. The air was warm.

As the Sun met the horizon and painted the landscape gold, the air began to cool, and The First Men decided to look for a place to build a fire. They knew how to build a fire because they were not from nowhere, and they are only the first men in *this* story.

The First Men worked together to find wood and build a fire. As the air cooled and the golden light turned blue, The First Men gathered around the fire.

When the Sun disappeared beneath the distant horizon, it took some of its warmth with it, and the fire — however small or shabby — provided light and warmth in place of the Sun.

As darkness settled in, the fire created a natural perimeter of light. The fire lit up a circle around it and whatever was above it — as far as the light of the fire could reach. Everything within the perimeter of light could be seen reasonably clearly, almost as if it were day.

Things that could be seen could be inspected and measured and evaluated. Things that moved could be watched, and the people inside the perimeter of light could observe the patterns in their movements. Things that threatened the health and the survival of the people inside the perimeter could be identified and neutralized or chased away. Things that could be used to sustain or improve the health and the quality of the lives of the people within the perimeter of light could be identified and used accordingly.

The First Men could see each others faces and gestures inside the perimeter of light. They were able to communicate as effectively as they could during the day.

Everything that was inside the perimeter of light around the fire could be comprehended, and everything that happened there was known. Inside the perimeter of light that surrounded the fire that The First Men built to replace the light and warmth of the Sun, the world was ordered. It made sense. And it was as safe as it could be.

The light of the fire flickered at the edges of this half sphere of illumination, and in the flickering light — in the threshold between light and darkness — there was a mystery of things half seen or seen only in part or only for a moment.

There was a space beyond the perimeter of illumination that was lit only by the light of the moon, which itself the reflected light of the Sun — though The First Men did not necessarily know this. In this space, in The Threshold, the light of the fire was still visible, and the way back to the fire was clear. From The Threshold, one could still see the fire in the dark — the central point from which all distances beyond were measured. The fire in the dark was the center of cosmos for The First Men - the central pole and axis around which their perception of order and meaning and identity revolved. Everything and everyone that The First Men truly cared about was close to the fire. One could say that the fire — the fire that the men built to replace the light and warmth of the sun — created its own "solar system."

Beyond the light of the fire and the cosmos of The First Men, there was only chaos. There was no visible point of orientation to which they could return, unless the way had been explored, and was known. Little could be seen, and what cannot be seen is unknown, and because it is unknown, it is out of order. Something could have had its own order and it may even have been able to see in the dark, but it would have been unknown and disordered to The First Men. If it moved, its patterns could not have been observed reliably. Perhaps it could not move at all - perhaps it was a cliff or a swamp or a patch of thorns. What is important to the story is that it could not be known, and that which cannot be comprehended or predicted or controlled...is chaos.

27

A fire can be a warning or a beacon, depending on the disposition of any particular creature "out there" in the chaotic realm of darkness. A fire may attract hungry animals, or Other Men.

The First Men relied on themselves, and could not expect help in an emergency. If their fire and the people and the culture and the ordered world they created around it were threatened by a creature from the realm of chaos and darkness beyond The Threshold, it would be up to The First Men to protect it — because no one else would.

And why would anyone else protect the fiery world that The First Men built? It was no one else's responsibility to keep their fire going, or to protect the people or the culture around it.

To protect the fire in the darkness and the ordered world from the chaos beyond it, The First Men needed to keep watch on the perimeter. When they sensed an external threat, it was their responsibility to overcome their fear of chaos, and venture out to the edges of the perimeter, into The Threshold and beyond, to investigate and ward off or eliminate that threat.

The First Men took turns watching the darkness through the night because it was part of their job to look out into the abyss.

After a few hours, the light began to change and the Sun returned to illuminate the void and render the wider world comprehensible.

The First Men looked up to the Sun, and were grateful for the day-lit sky.

"In the beginning was the Word,
and the Word was with God,
and the Word was God.
The same was in the beginning with God.
All things were made by him;
and without him was not any thing made that was made.
In him was life; and the life was the light of men.
And the light shineth in darkness; and the darkness comprehended it
not."

— John 1:1-5. *The King James Bible*

COSMOS

κόσμος

Ancient Greek. Order, lawful order, world, universe. Descended from the Proto-Indo-European root *Ḱens-, meaning to put in order or to "proclaim solemnly."[9] Related to Sanskrit शंसति (śáṃsati), meaning to declare, announce, proclaim, praise, or commend.

28

A campfire is a microcosm, a tiny cosmos that illustrates the way that man interacts with chaos, imposes his own order, and alters his environment — to aid in his survival, but also in accordance with his own vision and will.

Every campfire is a miniature imitation of the sun. When man builds a fire — when he builds his own sun — he imitates the work of a patriarchal god. He starts a world. He fathers a tiny order. The reach of the fire's light creates a logical system — a semi-spherical zone within which the world is intelligible and known and separate from the darkness and the unknown. The light symbolizes order and reason and the known world. Every campfire creates a culture, influenced by the men and women around it and the world around them and how they interpret it. The perimeter of light illuminates the order that man wants to protect from disorder. If the light goes out, the ordered world slips back into disorder and "chaos reigns."

29

> *"To you, Agni, who shine upon darkness, we come day after day, bringing our thoughts and homage*
> *to you, the king over sacrifices, the shining guardian of the Order, growing in your own house.*
> *Be easy for us to reach, like a father to his son. Abide with us, Agni, for our happiness."*

— *The Rig Veda*

According to some Vedic traditions, the construction of a fire altar is necessary to validate the possession of a new territory.[10]

Agni is the god of sacred fire, and it is through him that man communicates with the divine. His name comes from $^*h_1 ng^w nis$, the same Proto-Indo-European root that produced the word "ignite" in the West.[11] It's a masculine word that indicates a fire that is active, to be distinguished from fire that is merely a naturally occurring phenomenon. Sacred fire is man-made, intentional fire. Our more common word, "fire," comes from the Proto-Indo-European root $^*péh_2 w\mathring{r}$, a neuter word which describes a common, "inactive" fire with no sacred quality.

Throughout human history, "eternal flames" have been lit and kept burning to symbolize continuity and memory. Eternal flames were ignited and fueled at the Temple of Delphic Apollo, in ancient Iran, in Solomon's Temple, and in the Temple of Vesta in Rome. Today, many "eternal flames" are kept burning in memorials, demonstrating a commitment to maintaining a connection to the past and honoring the dead. Of course, none of these eternal flames have lasted or will last forever. They are extinguished or allowed to go out when the cultures associated with them become irrelevant or the people who tended them disappear or fall from power. These fires are sacred symbols of cultural identities, of stories about reality, of words and orders created by men. When the fire goes out, the story ends.

30

In Sanskrit, the word "mandala" मण्डल essentially means "circle" or "disc" and it ultimately comes from a Proto-Indo-European root that means "to turn." Over time, the word acquired many meanings, including "a path of orbit," and the "halo around the sun or moon." Each book in *The Rig Veda* is also called a mandala. You may recognize the word mandala as an elaborate circular design, because over time, various sects of Hindus and Buddhists developed the idea of a mandala as a tool for depicting a reality — an entire universe, a cosmos, a microcosm, or the conceptualization of a god. Mandalas became a religious art form, and have been used for centuries as tools for meditation and the depiction of esoteric ideas. Carl Jung became fascinated with mandalas, and experimented with them in psychology, drawing individual mandalas and having patients draw them to explore and harmonize their inner and outer worlds.

An intentional, sacred fire creates its own mandala. When man builds a fire, he creates a self-contained circular world of light that draws attention in toward its center.

31

Even a recreational campfire has much in common with the

primitive survival fire and the sacred, intentional fire that represents the beginning of a new order or culture. People go camping in many cases to have some version of the same experience they've been having for a few hundred thousand years. They create a home away from home and the fire provides light and warmth. People in groups sitting around fires tell stories and by the time they leave, they have probably exchanged ideas and shared a few jokes and experiences that are unique to that group around that particular fire.

An actual fire is not required to reproduce the process of cosmogony. In imitation of the gods, man harnessed the power of lightning, and we now have electric and portable lights. We reorganize spaces and create rules and within them when we rent or buy a new home or start a new business.

Like burrowing animals or birds building nests, when men decide to settle in a place, they change it. They use the natural resources they find around them to build shelters and tools and weapons to help them survive and to make themselves more comfortable. They move stones and bend and break the branches of trees and clear out undesirable plants and other animals.[12] Men may designate separate areas around the camp for sleeping, for cooking, and for waste.

When men build a camp, they reorganize the natural world, make use of it, and impose their own order on it. Men envision and work to create an oasis of order in the midst of a chaotic expanse.

Men have called this cosmic sanctuary a settlement, a *tkóymos*, a *haimaz*, a heim, a ham, and a home.

A home is a piece of the natural world that you have reordered in a way that serves, comforts and pleases you. Your home is a place that you know better than any other. When you leave, home is your point of origin and the place you return to.

As the power and influence of man increases, the realm upon which he can impose his order expands. Man improves his camp, and therefore improves his position in his environment, solidifying the extent of his control. The camp is fortified to become a fort, and the expanded fort becomes a castle. Castles are built upon castles, cities upon cities in cycles of continual improvement and refinement.

When one looks over the earth from the sky, man's careful and geometric reordering of the natural world is plainly evident and, in its way, often beautiful.

Though, it must be said that "improvement" itself is somewhat subjective and situational and is itself subject to revision and improvement. What seems like a better idea at a given time may turn out to create unforeseen problems, or even chaos.

32

Men are not creatures who merely experience life. We are at our least human and most animalistic — at our lowest and worst — when we are merely reacting to stimuli. Our sacred gift is consciousness and our consciousness wants to understand and reason and organize.

Scientific inquiry is a continuation of primal man's investigation of the components of his environment around him — rendering the unknown, known, and converting chaos into cosmos.

Scientists investigate, observe, classify, and give names.

There is nothing in the world that needs a name to exist. It is man who gives names to things so that he can organize the material world and organize his own mind. To give a thing a name is to place it in array.

In a state of chaos, everything is unknown and therefore undifferentiated.

Names and definitions differentiate. To say that a thing is a "tree" differentiates it from a "bush" or a "rock" and also excludes it from being a "bush" or a "rock." A tree can be a type, or sub-classification of the name "plant." Men differentiate one sort of action from another action, one sort of emotional feeling from another emotional feeling, one sort of sickness from another sickness, one sort of sensation from another sensation.

The process of imposing order on one's environment always involves the sorting of objects and creatures and sensations and actions. Vocabulary is a taxonomy of all things.

"In the beginning was the Word..."

And the word "Word" in that particular instance was actually a translation of the Greek logos, which also means "reason" and "logic."

The way in which men choose to sort and order and name experiences and aspects of their environment tells a story about their perspective. Naming is storytelling. If men were to number things instead of naming them, that would also tell a story about their perspective.

Naming is also rule-making. To declare that "this" is not "that" is to make a rule about what is right and agreed upon.

Changing the name of a thing changes the rule and the story and the order of things. This makes the names of things extremely important to the orders of men.

33

Words and language and drawings are used to tell stories about both our outer and inner worlds. Our stories about the world become part of our orders, and the stories shared within our perimeters, with those included in our particular orders, become the axes of our shared identities. The group that is "us" is united by stories about the world, and by stories about "us."

These stories can be mythological, philosophical or political. These stories become so sacred to men that men will sometimes fight to preserve an idea — a story — at the expense of their own safety or the safety of members of their group.

34

The English words "rule" and "ruler" and many words that describe the role or person of a king all descend from a common Indo-European root, *$h_3reǵ$-, which meant "to straighten or right." Its extension, *$h_3réǵ$-s, became the Latin *rēx* — still used in the royal styles of some European kings and queens —the Sanskrit राजन् (*rájan*) and the proto-Celtic *rīxs, the descendants of which became words for king in Old Irish, Old Welsh, and Scottish Gaelic.

It is the job of a king or ruler to "straighten things out," and the word ruler also describes a tool we'd use to draw a straight line. Rules are lines that must not be crossed, boundaries between what is lawful and what is outlawed, between what is permitted inside the perimeter of order, and what must be banished to the chaos outside in the name of order. Rules differentiate, and keep all things from blending together, becoming one, and returning to an undifferentiated state of chaos.

A king draws and keeps lines — straight lines — that extend outward like lines of longitude from a central, sacred point.

That sacred point is the point of *hierophany*, the *axis mundi* that connects man and earth with his highest ideals.

Hierophany combines the Greek word *hierós* (ἱερός)[13], an adjective which indicates that something is sacred, holy or connected to the gods, with the word *phaínō* (φαίνω), a verb that means "to reveal" or "to bring to light."

From the same root, hierós, comes the word hierarchy, which essentially means "holy rule." *Árkhō* (ἄρχω) means, "to lead, rule, govern or command." Our modern interpretation of the word hierarchy describes an order in which one thing or person is ranked highest, and all other things or people are ranked in descending order beneath it. Like lines of latitude, lines of hierarchy mark out steps of distance from the pole of what men value as highest, farthest North, and most sacred.

There is a Proto-Indo-European root, $*h_2er$-, that meant, "to fix" or "to put together." Through its extensions $*h_2er$-d^h- and $*h_2or$-d^h-$H\bar{o}$, we get the Latin word ordō, describing an arrangement or group, which became our English word order. Through its extension $*h_2rtós$, comes the Latin artus, meaning fitted, and the Sanskrit ऋत *r̥tá*, meaning "fixed or settled order," "truth," "divine truth," "sacred action or custom," and "right or righteousness." ऋत *R̥tá* is probably the most perfect and compact word that describes the concept of "sacred order." Finally, from another extension of $*h_2er$-, $*h_2reh_1$-, words have come down to us that mean to reckon, to reason, to decide and, most importantly, the Greek word that means goodness, excellence, and virtue: ἀρετή (areté).

The latitudinal steps of hierarchy can be viewed as measures of relative excellence, degrees of "areté" that indicate distance from or proximity to the divine ideal.

35

We have been seeking that which is sacred to men.

If there is one unifying and universal concept that is fundamental to the nature of man, a superordinate condition that he is compelled to create wherever he goes, something that a righteous man will fight to defend and struggle to maintain to his last breath, it is order.

The order is the fire, man's re-creation of the sun and its light — kindled and kept burning to stave off the horror of darkness and chaos.

The gods and heroes and ideals that man has elevated highest over and over again are primarily concerned with the creation, the championing and the perpetuation of order.

The god who creates and oversees order, the hero who fights to protect or expand order, the worldly lord of fertility who manipulates the material world to perpetuate order — these are the lights, the fires that have burned longer than any flame intended to be eternal. They are gods that represent the highest and most necessary work of men.

In the works of Homer, the Olympian gods are referred to as "the deathless ones." Men prayed and sacrificed to the gods in hope that the gods would favor them and touch and guide their lives in the way that the gods touched and guided the lives of the mythic heroes. They deferred to higher and more perfect forms of themselves, and hoped to draw from them a little more strength, a little more courage, a little more inspiration and ingenuity to help them overcome the challenges of both extraordinary situations and their everyday lives.

These "deathless" forms have been renamed and reshaped and

their myths have been rewritten and retold, with details added and subtracted. There have been elaborations and redistributions of labor across the pantheons. However, the fundamental cosmic principles are transcendent. Man's nature and his eternal struggle against chaos remains constant.

People often speak of "forces of nature." The god concepts or archetypes that I am reintroducing are forces within man's nature — externalized and made sacred. They are the essential pieces of the divine in man, united by the ordering principle of solar fire.

These gods have had many names, and they have been divided and reimagined in a thousand ways throughout the ages. From the high seat of our time that overlooks all time, I have reintegrated them into a primal triad: The Father, The Striker, and the Lord of the Earth. It is a tripartite system that idealizes the way that man creates, champions, and perpetuates his cosmos in his eternal struggle to overcome chaos.

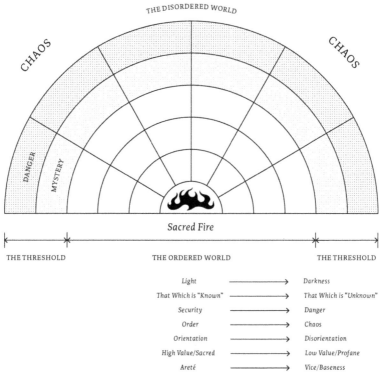

THE DISORDERED WORLD

CHAOS

CHAOS

DANGER

MYSTERY

Sacred Fire

THE THRESHOLD   THE ORDERED WORLD   THE THRESHOLD

Light	⟶	Darkness
That Which is "Known"	⟶	That Which is "Unknown"
Security	⟶	Danger
Order	⟶	Chaos
Orientation	⟶	Disorientation
High Value/Sacred	⟶	Low Value/Profane
Areté	⟶	Vice/Baseness

Natural Path of Entropy, Disorder, & Dissolution

⟶

CREATE ~ CHAMPION ~ PERPETUATE

The Tripartite System

36

This is a spiritual book, and it is the product of both theory and practice.

The integrated, tripartite system that I am presenting is not solely based in theories developed over books and keyboards, but is also the product of ritual art, practice, and meditation. Some of these words and ideas came to me in candlelight and I shouted them out over a roaring fire back into the void, surrounded by dead-serious men covered in ash and their own blood.

So, to introduce and explain this system, I'm going to take you back to that fire in the dark — to my own sacred circle where this order first revealed itself to me.

ODIN ~ THOR ~ FREY

37

At the beginning of 2018, I was performing Germanic pagan rituals for a small group of men at Waldgang — five acres of lichen-covered oaks and ponderosa pines in the dry, rocky hills of Southeastern Washington near the Columbia River Gorge. Each month I spent several days researching the concept of the next ritual and meditating on it as I wrote it out and committed parts of it to memory. By this point, I had already been performing group rituals like this every month for several years.

I started the year as I often had with Ymirblot, a sacrifice honoring Odin's murder of the monstrous, pre-conscious beast Ymir. Odin committed this act with his brothers, Villi and Vé, whose names mean something like "will" and "a sacred space" in Old Norse. Odin's name (PG - *wodanaz*) is derived from roots that mean "fury" or "inspiration" or "madness." (ON - Óðr; PG - *wodaz*) The functions of the brothers are all in their names. "Fury, Will, and Sanctity" is another tripartite system — a formula for initiating the magic of creation. In the lore related to this sacrifice, Odin made a new world — his own order — from the corpse of a creature that was by all accounts chaotic and possibly evil in nature. I had already performed a ritual sacrifice[14] on this theme several times by this point, and it had always been one of my favorites, because it is a story of violent cosmogenesis — of Odin "starting the world," which has been a thematic interest and a slogan of mine since I wrote *The Way of Men*.

Toward the end of that month, uncertain about the theme for the next ritual, I camped out at Waldgang overnight. I performed a short ritual, ate some mushrooms, and then bundled up in the "black box" bunkhouse as a light January snow fell outside. During the night, my mind fixed on the idea of an organic darkness and it occurred to me that Odin's magic drew on dark, chaotic forces that were older than he was. In his creation of the world from the body of Ymir, he was taking something old and dark and reshaping it to serve his own ends. He was reordering an ancient, unconscious chaos, or reordering an alien order — depending on how you want to look at it. The next month, I wrote and conducted a strange ritual focused on "the darkness" and its relationship to the creation of order.

Our group at the time agreed that the next ritual should honor Thor, and following this theme — the creation of order — it became obvious to me that Thor should be invoked as a protector of the order that Odin created.[15] Thor embodies the archetypal role of the thumotic warrior, the auxiliary enforcer of the Platonic "guardian" class. He was especially beloved by the common folk and seen as a hero of the people. He slays jotnar[16] (or "giants"), strange and powerful outsiders who threaten the order of men and gods.

As April approached we were all looking forward to spring, and as in previous years, we planned a "charming of the plow" ritual dedicated to the god Frey, at an altar we'd constructed especially for him. Frey is associated with love and fecundity and the cycles of nature. His name in Old Norse and in earlier forms means "lord," and he is also associated with lordship. By this time, I'd come to identify Frey with a certain worldliness and the daily work of managing people and wealth, distinguished from the higher functions of the sacred king, which in the late Old Norse lore would be attributed to Odin as world-creator and ruler of Asgard.

In The Ynglinga Saga, a far different and more euhemeristic interpretation of the myths, Odin was a mortal warrior-sorcerer who founded a kingdom and gave laws. After a war with the people of Vanaheim, he made Njord and his son Frey — two of the best men of Vanaheim - priests of his order. After Odin died, Njord and later Frey ruled his kingdom. So, in this context, in addition to his association with fertility, Frey *perpetuates* Odin's order.

After authoring and performing that ritual cycle, this system articulating the creation, defense, and perpetuation of order ascended in my mind and became my primary framework for perceiving and understanding the roles of the most prominent gods in the Germanic pantheon.

One of the functions of a priest or a spiritual leader is to make myth relevant and relatable to laymen. It is his role to inspire men, and to suggest answers to the question, "how do I apply this lesson or ideal to my life?" Religion is "spiritual technology," and in order for men to want to make it part of their lives, it has to be useful and applicable. That technology has to *work*. It has to make their internal lives better in some palpable albeit abstract way.

When I wrote these rituals, this was also my purpose. When I spoke about Odin confronting a chaotic being and destroying it to create a new order from its remains, a question that followed naturally was, "what do you have to destroy in your own life to create the new order you want?" When I invoked Thor to talk about strength and courage and a willingness to protect order, questions that followed were, "What are you going to do to build strength and courage? How are you going to defend your order?" When I talked about Frey and perpetuating the cycles of life and the natural world, I asked, "What are the things you need to do to keep what you have —to keep it alive, to keep it going?"

Having asked similar questions many times, I recognized that these three functions — the creation of order, the defense of order, and the protection of order — were not merely roles that different men filled, or different types of men. These three functions are relevant to all men in some way, and describe roles that most of us will perform or attempt to perform over and over again throughout our lives.

It occurred to me that this was not only a workable model of social orders or gods, but of masculine lives and the male psyche itself. Over time, these external orders and roles shaped the way we perceive our internal reality, and vice-versa. The role of the warrior/guardian who defends and expands order is the role of the man who defends the perimeter. It is the role of the man who hunts and fights with the "gang" or war band that I wrote about in *The Way of Men*.

For some time before and during that year, I was also realizing some of the limits of Germanic practice in a contemporary context. The available source material is extremely limited when compared to what is known about other ancient religions, and the majority of the primary documents were written down for the first time and interpreted by Christians. A problem with most forms of contemporary neopaganism is that they are rooted in a fixed period of time that has already passed, and in many cases — especially for Americans — a foreign place. Instead of living in the present, the tendency is to engage in an escapist form of creative anachronism. Further, while there are good eggs for certain, many of the people drawn to Germanic paganism or heathenry are often either wrapped up in some new-agey post-Wiccan nature worship, or obsessed with preserving what they believe to be their racial heritage, or, weirdly (though this is very often the case) — both. The bulk of the quality writing on Germanic neopaganism is also heavily influenced by occultists and mystics of the late 19th and early 20th Century and is peppered with the prevailing political and cultural fixations of that era.

The Way of Men said things that were true about and for men from every ethnic and racial background, and I wanted to ally myself with men who were interested in the same kind of strength-based culture and myth, but who were not necessarily or particularly "Germanic." My thinking was moving in a broader direction, and I was more interested in evaluating the men around me according to their individual excellences and virtues — according to areté and general affinity — without first investigating their family trees.

As I stepped back and took a wider view and did more research, I connected this personal articulation of the functions of the Germanic gods to their roles in Dumézil's trifunctional system.

SOVEREIGN - MILITARY - PRODUCTIVE

38

Georges Dumézil was a philologist — a scholar who studies language, particularly in historical texts. His studies compared the mythologies and social orders of Indo-European cultures.

Indo-European cultures are all related linguistically, although the people who spoke and still speak Indo-European languages are not necessarily related genetically in any significant way.

Words are a taxonomy of all things, and the way we choose to name things often tells a story about the way in which we perceive and contextualize objects and phenomena and abstractions. Words have their own stories, but they are obviously also used to tell stories. So, myth often travels with language.

There are myths that are found in some form in almost every culture, and archetypal themes that could almost be called human universals.[17] For instance, the dualism that associates women with the darkness, the earth, water and chaos, and associates men with the daylight, the sun, fire and order, is found in the Far East in the form of Yin and Yang as well as throughout Indo-European mythology.

However, because ideas and stories travel with language, as cultures separate and distinguish themselves from one another, Indo-European stories seem to repeat the same patterns in a way that seems to indicate that, as with Indo-European languages, they evolved from a common source.

Dumézil is known best for his "trifunctional hypothesis" regarding the structure of Indo-European societies. While Dumézil is seen as a controversial figure by some, his trifunctional model has endured and is referenced throughout the field of Indo-European studies by contemporary scholars like J.P. Mallory. Based mainly on mythological themes, Dumézil proposed that the people of Indo-European cultures were socially divided into a hierarchy according to three main functions: sovereignty, military, and productivity.

The sovereign function would have included priests and kings, the originators and overseers of legal and spiritual order. Dumézil believed that the sovereign role was a dual role often filled mythologically by two complementary deities or individuals. One aspect of the sovereign was magical and creative and maybe a little crazy, while the other was primarily concerned with justice, rules, and organization.[18]

The military function obviously refers to the work of the warrior class — the men who were charged with defending and in some cases expanding order.

The productive function was filled by farmers, herders, craftsmen, traders, and all those whose labors ensured the sustenance of all of the classes and the perpetuation of order.

Having written extensively about masculinity and various men's movements, I was already familiar with the system of masculine archetypes popularized by Robert Moore in his book *King, Warrior, Magician, Lover*, and I recognized many common and overlapping themes between his system and Dumézil's trifunctional system.

KING/MAGICIAN - WARRIOR - LOVER

39

Psychoanalyst Robert Moore and his collaborator Douglas Gillette popularized a Jungian shuffle of the same masculine roles in their book, *King, Warrior, Magician, Lover* (1990)— with a holistic exploration of the male psyche specifically in mind. Moore and other members of the mythopoetic men's movement of the period, like Robert Bly, were focused on what they correctly recognized as a crisis in masculine identity.

They attributed this crisis largely to an absence of male initiations. I'll argue that the absence of initiation was itself an effect of a collapse of cultural homogeneity and collective agreement about the role and responsibilities associated with being an adult male. You can't initiate young men into a role if no one agrees on what exactly that role is. There is more confusion about this today than ever now that young people are encouraged by the media and their activist-educators to feign uncertainty about their gender identity, and are rewarded for doing so with a status of both distinction and honored victimhood. What Moore called the "veritable blitzkrieg on the male gender" has only intensified, as has the "outright demonization of men and a slander against masculinity."[19] I do not expect to see anything approaching a mainstream national or global consensus on a positive male role in my lifetime.

If there are to be meaningful initiations into manhood, they will have to take place within small communities of like-minded parents. Initiations into roles within private groups for men are also possible and valid, but men will have to actively create, defend, and perpetuate new, syncretic traditions and standards. It is my hope that the ideas in this book will assist them in that process.

King, Warrior, Magician, Lover uses the same broad archetypes as Dumézil,[20] with the dual role of the jurist sovereign and the magical sovereign separated out into King and Magician archetypes. Moore advanced the idea that these archetypes were all present in every man, and relevant in some way and at some time to every man's life. *King, Warrior, Magician, Lover*, and supporting texts from Moore have been extremely influential over the past 30 years for a wide range of men interested in exploring masculine psychology and spirituality. His explanations of the archetypes are worth reading. His thoughts on what it means to be a good King are especially compelling and relevant to this book.

The King, according to Moore, has two functions: ordering and providing fertility or blessing. The King is an exemplar, living in "right order" as his people are expected to live—in accordance with their morals and traditions. Theoretically, if he fails to live in right order, misfortune befalls the kingdom. Moore referred to the King as the primary archetype for all men, and states that, "... the King archetype comes close to being God in his masculine form within every man."[21]

The Warrior is, "universally present in us men and in the civilizations we create, defend, and extend. It is a vital ingredient in our world-building and plays an important role in extending the benefits of the highest human virtues and cultural achievements to all of humanity."[22] Moore acknowledged but was obviously uncomfortable with the Warrior's connection to violence. His ideal warrior was a self-sacrificing ascetic, ready to die at any moment for a cause beyond himself. He acknowledged that warrior energy is aggressive and pointed out that, "aggressiveness is a stance toward life that rouses, energizes, and motivates."[23] Moore distinguished the Warrior from the Hero, whom he associated with grandstanding, childishness, and fantasyland foolishness.

The Magician "understands the links between the unseen world of the spirits—the Divine World—and the world of human beings and nature." The Magician is, "confessor and priest. He is the one who can think through the issues that are not obvious to other people. He is a seer and a prophet in the sense not only of predicting the future but also of seeing deeply."[24] Moore also saw the Magician as a guide for the King archetype, like Merlin for King Arthur, and this is a productive way to envision the relationship between the two aspects of Dumézil's magical and jurist kings. One deals with darkness, mystery, and the occult (hidden) world, and the other *applies* that wisdom, knowledge, and understanding in the material world of daylight. Moore identified the shadow or negative aspect of the magician as the spiritual adviser who conceals his intentions and uses his knowledge and talent to manipulate those who trust him.

The Lover is a passionate empath and a sensualist. In his fullness, he brings joy to life with his appreciation for beauty and love, and this is the aspect of man who connects best with women and family and friends. The shadow of this epicurean empath is the addict who loses sight of his purpose and his responsibilities while chasing love or lust or some other sensual addiction like food, drink, or drugs.

Much of *King, Warrior, Magician, Lover* is devoted to contrasting "mature" masculinity with "boy psychology," and Moore makes some valid observations in this realm. He explains negative elements of the archetypes in boy psychology and connects them to their "shadow" counterparts in adult male archetypes.

However, Moore's work was handicapped by his feminism and his politics. He agreed with his progressive academic and therapeutic peers that patriarchy was evil and oppressive, and argued that patriarchy — really any dominant masculinity — was an "immature" expression of masculinity, although he admitted that "there never has been a time yet in human history when mature masculinity (or mature femininity) was really in ascendancy."

Something is wrong with your definition of "maturity" if men have never been "mature" in all of human history.

Arguably, all successful tribal cultures and civilizations — meaning, the groups we know about because they weren't wiped out and completely erased from history — have been patriarchal. The King, Warrior, Magician, and Lover archetypes are all products of patriarchal societies, just as Dumézil's three functions in myth and social order are also the products of patriarchal societies. The fact that this made Moore uncomfortable due to his devotion to a novel, anti-historical, and fundamentally anti-human ideology doesn't make it any less true.

THE CHARIOT OF THE SOUL

40

The philosopher Plato developed his own tripartite structures that match up nicely with the divisions of Dumézil, the three primary Germanic gods, and Moore's archetypes.

In his dialog titled *Phaedrus*, Plato described the soul as a chariot pulled by two winged horses in the context of a discussion about love. One of horses was of "noble" origin and the other was of "ignoble" origin, and his assertion was that they must be whipped and reigned in by a careful and conscientious charioteer.

He described love as a divine madness in which you catch a glimpse of a beauty that is eternal in another person. The noble horse wants to proceed toward that person in the name of beauty and righteousness, so it is easily persuaded by a reasonable charioteer. In contrast, the ignoble horse is wild and base and lusty, and it wants to rush in recklessly to satisfy its hunger — so it has to be reigned in and punished. His point was that love, this divine madness, could only be fruitful and positive if both horses were tamed and guided by logic and reason.

41

In *Republic*, Plato expands on this idea of the tripartite soul and relates it to the social classes of his ideal city-state. He separates men into three categories or classes — Guardians, Guardian Warriors, and a productive class. Each social class or role is characterized by a particular quality that could in theory be moderated or become dangerously excessive.

The Guardians, or counsellors, are the men who Plato believed should rule — men who demonstrate a love for wisdom and goodness and truth and right order. They are frequently referred to as "philosopher kings." The guardians are the charioteers of the city, and they are characterized by *logos* — logic and reason. The Guardians are chosen from among the class of Guardian Warriors, who are educated as if they may one day become Guardians.

The Guardian Warriors, or auxiliaries, are the protective class of men, who enforce order within the city and defend it from external threats. The Guardian Warriors can be likened to the chariot's "noble horse," and they are characterized by *thumos*, or "high spiritedness." Thumos has come to be associated with emotional anger, an emotional desire to be recognized or respected, an emotional reaction to perceived injustice, and in its noblest form, the emotion that — coupled with courage — drives men to acts of heroism and self-sacrifice. However, when unchecked it can lead to fury, unproductive outbursts, and bloodlust.

The Productive Class includes traders, craftsmen, farmers, and basically everyone else. The Productive Class makes the other classes possible, and it also makes them necessary. The Productive Classes work to satisfy everyone's basic needs and material wants. As such, for Plato, they were characterized by appetite (epithymetikon).

Appetites are connected to our mortality and our humanity. They are essential drives that spur us to eat, to seek shelter, to procreate. Our basic needs must be met in order for us to survive, and much of the joy in life comes from overindulging these needs in some way. We can survive on nutritious gruel, but we enjoy fine food. We can survive in tents, but most would rather live in a more comfortable home. We only need to have sex a few times in our lives to procreate, but most of us would prefer to do it more often. The productive classes help us meet and exceed these natural desires, but it is in the nature of man to always want more of something, and when unregulated, our natural drives can consume us and become counterproductive or destructive.

Perhaps this connection to mortality and carnal need is why Plato wrote in *Phaedrus* that while man has one noble horse and one horse "of ignoble origin," the souls of the immortal gods were carried by two noble horses.

42

Plato's Guardian, Guardian Warrior, and Productive classes match up closely with Dumézil's trifunctional hypothesis and the King/Magician, Warrior, Lover system. His three parts of the soul that also correspond to his three social classes — characterized by logos, thumos and appetite — provide a useful model for evaluating differences between the three primary ideals that correspond to natural divisions and tendencies within the masculine psyche and the different kinds of roles a man will be called to fill over the course of his life.

CREATE - CHAMPION - PERPETUATE

43

Dumézil connected the myths of Indo-European societies to what he believed to be their three main social orders and functions. *King, Warrior, Magician, Lover* links essentially the same mythic structures and archetypes to masculine psychology and the inner world of men. Through reason and philosophical discussion, Plato created a tripartite model of the soul and divided the social classes of his ideal city-state into three parts according to the primary roles he concluded were necessary, and the characteristics that best served each role.

Because we can sit in our high seats and look out over history with all of the information in the world at our fingertips, we can see the links and the unity and the continuity and the harmony between all of these mythic, functional, social, and psychological forms. The sovereign/military/productive is Odin/Thor/Frey and King-Magician/Warrior/Lover.

Comparative mythologists from Bulfinch to Frazer to Campbell and so many Jungians like Moore have made important contributions to human understanding by tying together ideas that once seemed alien to and different from each other. They connected the threads, and recognizable patterns have emerged. It also seems that Plato recognized the same patterns.

Recently, my friend Ryan Michler, host of the extremely popular and well-respected podcast "The Order of Man," popularized the motto "Protect, Provide, Preside," through his book, *Sovereignty*. Like many well-known advocates for masculinity, Michler is a Mormon, and I pointed out to him on a podcast that his motto also conceptually lines up with the tripartite systems explored above. The King/Sovereign/Guardian presides. The Warrior/ Military/Guardian Warrior aspect of man protects or champions.

The Lover/Productive part of man serves natural appetites by providing for the people around him and perpetuating life. Despite our different backgrounds and approaches, Michler and I are for the most part seeing and saying the same things about the masculine mind and the roles of men.

Men keep seeing the same patterns, the same roles, the same ideals, the same key features of the masculine psyche over and over again. There's something consistent — something eternally true about this tripartite division. It's been around for a long time and it's bigger than all or any of us.

44

Systems are all stories about the worlds around us and within us. Men develop systems to provide some order — a rough framework to help us make sense of our surroundings, emotions, and experiences.

I have spent years pondering and writing about the nature of men, and listening to what men today say they want and watching what they respond to. I've looked at the systems above and researched many of the myths and epics and fragments from the past that inspired them. We cannot return to the past or live in it. We are alive right now, and this is our time, and we find ourselves sitting in our high seats looking out over the entire history of mankind.

We live in a world where, for many, god is dead. We live in a time of disorder, where all values are in question and flux. We live in a sprawling, global Empire of Nothing, where so many thumb-suckers want to or have already returned to the womb, to the void, to sleep in a space where all is one and chaos is queen.

Now is a time for reintegration and synthesis, for cosmogenesis and theogony.

Beginning with a single, solar point of fire in the dark, using all of this kindling from the past, I've created a new pantheon for the present. A system of three ideals for men, renamed and faced forward, outward into the unknown darkness. Three to light the way of men, as we venture into the future.

45

THE FATHER

The Father creates order and presides over it. He represents Dumézil's dualistic sovereign, overcoming conceptual chaos and ensuring right and just order. The Father integrates aspects of Moore's King and Magician archetypes. Rex, rājan, and ruler, he straightens things out and draws lines from the solar point of hierophany that differentiate and establish hierarchies of meaning and value. He is Plato's Guardian, his truth and wisdom-loving philosopher king and counsellor, the charioteer of men and every man's soul, characterized by logos. He is not the sun, but he is highest and closest to it, and shares much in common with it.

The Germanic people called him Odin the "Allfather," the Greeks called him Zeus, the Latins called him Jupiter, and in most systems, he has ruled from the sky as an ascended warrior. According to Dumézil, in the Vedic sources he is represented in some aspects by *Mitra-Varuna*, principle guardian(s) of truth and order (ṛtá).

THE STRIKER

The Striker is the idealized hero who fights physical forces of chaos to protect or expand the perimeter of light and order created and maintained by The Father. He is the lightning bolt, the striking force hurled outward to the edge of the perimeter. Without the Striker, order cannot survive, and his virtues are the primary survival virtues of masculinity — Strength, Courage, Mastery and Honor. He epitomizes Dumézil's military function and Moore's Warrior. Like Plato's Guardian Warriors or auxiliaries, he protects the sacred order from within as well as without. He enforces the rules of the ruler. The Striker is characterized by thumos.

The Germanics called him Thor, and the Latins called him Mars. Among the Greeks, The Striker was represented by Ares, but also the gods who slew chaotic beasts, as with Apollo and Python. The Striker was also represented by the myriad heroes typified by the club-wielding Herakles — half son of father Zeus. In the Vedas, he is Indra. The Celts knew him as Taranis, and as a hero, he is typified by the Irish Cú Chulainn.

THE LORD OF THE EARTH

The Lord of the Earth represents the earthly, mortal aspect of man, and his function is to contend with and manage the material chaos of the natural world in order to produce that which is necessary to sustain life, and to perpetuate life itself through fertility. In Dumézil's system, he fulfills the Productive function, and among Moore's archetypes, he is best represented by the Lover. The Lord of the Earth is the exemplar of Plato's farmers, craftsmen, and traders. He is characterized by appetite — by Freudian "Id." However, when the three aspects of man are working in harmony, these appetites are well-managed and restrained in accordance with the order of The Father.

The Germanics knew him as Freyr. While little is known about the early Celtic gods, Teutātes and the horned god Cernunos both seem to have fulfilled aspects of his functions. Among the Greeks, the idealized craftsman was Hephaestus, the blacksmith of the gods, while the wine god Dionysus and various rustic gods like Pan inspired carnal pleasure and fertility. In the Rig Veda, The Lord was represented by Pūṣan, "the nourisher" — a god of shepherds, marriages, roads, and wealth.

46

In the following chapters, I'll flesh out the natures and qualities of these three ideals, connect them to ideals and exemplars from the past, and reconcile them with the tripartite systems above.

These three ideals transcend the limitations of time, place, and heritage. This integrated pantheon also overcomes the problem of incomplete or questionable source material. The Father encompasses all fathers — all kings and leaders. The Striker is the archetypal warrior, the epitome of all heroes. The Lord of the Earth represents every fertility god, the highest version of every man who works or manages the land and makes use of natural resources to perpetuate life and bring joy to himself and the men and women around him. The source material is nearly limitless, and this framework provides a starting point for lifetimes of study, contemplation, and understanding that I can only gesture toward here. This pantheon is relevant and accessible to all men, because each of these ideals represent a distinct and eternal part of our natures, our experience, and our role in the world. These ideal forms exemplify aspects of our psyches connected to the eternal tasks of man — to create, champion, and perpetuate order in the midst of chaos. For all time, wherever we are and wherever we go, it has always been our purpose and our passion, to build fire in the dark.

PANTHEON

"The most popular prayer in the world is addressed to 'Our Father who art in heaven.' It is possible that man's earliest prayers were addressed to the same heavenly father."

— Mircea Eliade, *Patterns in Comparative Religion*

THE FATHER

Creator of Order

47

When a man is still a boy, he looks upward to his father as an exemplar. His father represents an ideal of man that towers above him and seems far beyond him.

To a female child, the father figure demonstrates what *a man* is and what *a man* does and how *a man* behaves.

The father figure shows the male child something about himself, about what *he* is. To a boy, the father figure is aspirational and signals the direction of his destiny — gestures at what he is and what he is in some way bound in time to become. The small and fragile child looks upward and imagines himself growing as tall and becoming as strong as his father, and one day becoming a father in his own right.

The father figure is a boy's first god, ordering and overseeing the household world of the child. He provides and protects and acts as the final arbiter of justice. Traditionally, a man's wife and children took his name and in some sense the identity of the family orbited around the identity of the father.

48

In Plato's "Analogy of the Sun," Socrates used the example of the sun to talk about the nature of goodness. [25] The sun is not generation or visibility itself, but it generates and makes visibility possible, so it is perhaps the best way we have to conceptualize generation and visibility. It is a shining symbol of the higher thing, the thing above and beyond itself. Likewise, Socrates explained, while goodness was not only the creator of the knowledge of things, but also of their being and essence, goodness itself was not essence, but something which far exceeded essence in dignity and power. Knowledge and being and essence were to goodness what the sun was to generation and visibility, in that they were the best way to conceptualize the nature of goodness, which — in Socrates' view — was beyond our comprehension (or at least his own).

If the father is the boy's first god, to understand the father and become a man himself, he must look beyond the person of his own father to conceptualize a higher ideal of what it means to be a man and a father. He cannot merely imitate his own father forever. He must conceptualize an ideal of what it means to be a father, a father above and beyond his own father. An ethereal and eternal father. *One father to rule them all.* An ..."allfather."

From the perspective of the boy looking upward to his own father and beyond him, it is easy to see how and why men across time and all around the world have so often envisioned their highest gods as fathers in the sky. Fathers above fathers, fathers who are greater than their own fathers, fathers who do what men and fathers do, on the grandest scale imaginable.

49

Odin, Zeus, Jupiter, and even the Biblical Jehovah are all father-creators and ordering forces in the sky — celestial judges overseeing the lives and the laws of gods and men.

Comparative mythologists and linguists have linked many of the sky-father concepts and constructed what they believe to be the name of a Proto-Indo-European progenitor god: Dyḗus ph₂tḗr, or, written more simply, Dyeus pəter. The name Dyeus — from which many of the romance languages derive their word for "god," such as the Latin "deus," the Spanish "dios" and the French "dieu" — comes from a Proto-Indo-European root that means "to shine." The name ph₂tḗr or pəter became the Latin "pater" and the early Germanic "*fadēr," and eventually the English word father. Proto-Indo-European language and religion would have originated around 5,000 years ago — give or take a millennium.

Not all sky fathers are directly descended linguistically or culturally from Dyeus pəter, but the fact that they have been found all around the world suggests something universal about human nature, and about the nature of men, and about their recurring experiences and perspectives. All around the world, women are associated with the earth, and men are associated with the sky, and in myth, the earth mother is the consort of the sky father. Dyḗus ph₂tḗr's proposed consort is *Dʰéǵʰōm Méh₂tēr, or "earth mother,' who is associated with fertility and possibly also the dead.

As social orders expand beyond the family unit, leaders, chieftains, kings and sometimes priests or priest-kings become "fathers beyond fathers" or "fathers of nations" or "spiritual fathers" who create and oversee order from a hierarchical position above the family father, but below the sky father. It has often been believed that this father-leader acted as an intermediary between earthly fathers and the sky father, with his authority derived from a blessing from the sky father, to whose sacred order he claimed to defer.

While any given reader may have a quarrel with the particular details of any given sky-father's established or written sacred order, the point here is to recognize the function of the father-as-leader, the leader-as-father, and the sky father above as the father-as-ideal.

50

The primary function of The Father is to contend with conceptual chaos. Characterized by logos, he uses reason to put the world in order, and to maintain that order.

The Father orients the world around the fire. He is not the fire, but conceptually, he is closest to it. He creates the point of reference and defines the perimeter. Within that perimeter, he is the final authority, although the earthbound father defers to the cosmic father — to his own highest ideal of what it means to be a father. He acts as a representative of the sun, or of all that the sun represents to men.

The bright light of the sun reveals truth, and the solar father on earth does his best to order his world in accordance with a sense of truth that is as close to being eternal and in harmony with his understanding of what is "right" as he is able to conceive. As such, his struggle is with concepts — with meaning and ideas. He acts as the primary determiner of names and narratives. He shapes the perception of reality around him by arranging, classifying and evaluating animals, objects, actions, emotions, experiences and thoughts.

The Father creates hierarchies of meaning and value, and oversees them to maintain their integrity.

"*I will proclaim the great magic of Varuna the famous Asura, who stood up in the middle realm of space and measured apart the earth with the sun as with a measuring stick.*"

— *The Rig Veda*

"...one must still have chaos in one, to give birth to a dancing star."

— Friedrich Nietzsche. Thus Spake Zarathustra.

THE FATHER IN DARKNESS AND LIGHT

51

It is the work of The Father to contend with and overcome conceptual chaos, and this conflict creates a duality in his nature. His outer persona is one of confidence, decisiveness, and certainty, as he oversees the sacred order which he has created or inherited. However, to create and maintain order, he must contend with and overcome confusions of meaning and value. To receive, discover, or determine the truth — to reach a conclusion — he must enter a realm of mystery and travel through it.

From a scientific perspective, we know that the sun is always in darkness. The sun travels through space, emanating light and warmth and pulling objects into gravitational orbits around it.

However, to the men who came before us, the sun disappeared at night. Men imagined that the sun went through its own ordeal, harrowing darkness from dusk until dawn, and emerging victorious every day. There is an echo of this imagining in the Roman concept of Sol Invictus, "the unconquerable sun," but it is perhaps best illustrated by the story of the Egyptian sun god, Ra.

52

Ra was believed to be the creator of the world and the king who reigned over all of the gods. His name was synonymous with the sun, and some have suggested that it also indicated "operative and creative power."[26] This god of the sun at noon was portrayed with the head of a high-flying hawk, crowned with a solar disc, encircled by a serpent.

Every night, Ra disappeared from the sky and journeyed through the underworld, Duat, on his evening barge. During this nightly voyage, the serpent Apep — known as the "Lord of Chaos" — attempts to stop the ship and, as a result, plunges the world into darkness and despair.

In Ancient Egypt, sacred truth, order, and wisdom were personified and regulated by Ra's daughter, the goddess Ma'at. As king of the gods and father of order, it was Ra's duty to protect order from the Lord of Chaos. With help from other gods, Ra defeats Apep, completes his nocturnal crossing, and is triumphantly reborn at dawn.

Ra is pictured as a hawk or a falcon during the daylight hours, but he is often shown with the head of a ram as he makes his way through the underworld. He has two principle aspects or faces — one glorious and exalted face that oversees the waking world, and another for overcoming chaos in a spirit realm of darkness and uncertainty.

53

The solar Sovereign has two sides. Dumézil made his case for dualism within the sovereign function beginning with the Vedic pairing of the solar deities Mitra–Varuna, who are both charged with the protection of Ṛta, cosmic order. In *The Rig Veda*, Mitra and Varuna are most often invoked together.[27]

While Mitra–Varuna are called together, usually as the guarantors of laws and pacts between men, it is Varuna who is treated with greater detail. In a recounting of his deeds, he is referred to as both king of kings and the creator of the world, who split the world in two and "placed the sun in the sky and the Soma on the mountain." [28] Dumézil also linked Varuna linguistically to Ouranós or Uranus, the Ancient Greek sky god who preceded Zeus. Varuna seems to be the more feared of the duo, whereas Mitra is associated with close friendship and he oversees covenants, contracts and oaths.[29]

In texts written after *The Rig Veda*, Varuna becomes increasingly associated with kingship and the night, whereas Mitra is associated with the sunrise and the priesthood. Beginning with this duality, Dumézil conducted a survey of Indo-European myths and religion, finding similar separations within the kingly and priestly ideals of Ancient Rome (Romulus and Numa), Iran (Ahura-Mazdah and Mithra), and finally the Germanic material (Odin and Tyr).

Dumézil characterized his assessment of the differences between the two roles most concisely here:

> "*Mitra is the sovereign under his reasoning aspect, luminous, ordered, calm, benevolent, priestly; Varuna is the sovereign under his attacking aspect, dark, inspired, violent, terrible, warlike.*"[30]

One aspect of the sovereign is associated with the public world "in the light of day," and the other delves into the wild, the supernatural, and the mysterious.

54

Dumézil argued that in the Germanic material, Odin (*wodanaz) represents the dark, warlike, and magical sovereign, while Tyr (*tiwaz) fulfills the judicial function — specifically, when he offered his arm to the wolf Fenrir to render the trickery of the gods who were coaxing him into bondage fair and "legal."[31] However, there are very few other surviving myths regarding Tyr/*tiwaz. While his name is a continuation of the Proto-Indo-European Dyếus, from what comparatively little is known about early Germanic culture, Tyr was rarely featured as one of the primary gods. Where Tyr is mentioned, he is described as a warrior known for great courage and invoked for victory in battle[32], which places him primarily within the military function as a warrior — as another manifestation of The Striker. Tyr also became a generic term for god, and the word "tyr" is used in kennings about Odin and other Germanic gods.

It seems to me that from the extant literature, if Odin and Tyr once shared the sovereign function, eventually Odin became a composite of the two roles, which is somewhat unique in Indo-European mythology.

While I believe that Odin was somewhat "demonized" by Christian interpreters, there are hints even in their works of both light and darkness — of an Olympian father as well as a magical war god of madness and inspiration. In Odin, we have a sky father who orders and presides over the gods, as well as a murdering creator, and a god who sacrifices himself to himself and rips out his own eye to better understand the nature of the universe.

55

The details of the attributes of The Father in Darkness and The Father in Light have varied from time to time and place to place — and all of the variations offer some insight — but the combination of both in one god, as with Odin, pulls back the curtain and reveals a more complete truth about the process of presiding over oneself and others.

When a man has resolved a problem or made a decision or chosen a way forward, he wants to project a calm confidence and certainty. He must convince himself and convince others that he has committed to his path.

In the most mythic sense, the sacred king or the prophet or the high priest experiences hierophany, where the divine speaks to him and through him. His word is the word of god — the word of The Father beyond fathers — by virtue of his position. He speaks *ex cathedra* — "from the chair" — as the Pope does, with presumed infallibility.

In everyday life, men sometimes prefer to believe that the men who they follow or admire simply are what they are and that they always know exactly the right thing to say or do. This is a pleasant illusion, and leaders often project this because it is what many people want to believe, and believing it makes people feel better. While some men do just seem to "know" the right ways to resolve difficult situations, if the situation is truly extraordinary or the matter is of grave importance, any conscientious leader will think more than twice about the problem, and question himself and struggle with all variables and potential outcomes before he makes his decision. He will have to work through some turmoil.

There are of course innumerable records of father gods and kings struggling with difficult decisions, but take an example from Homer's *Iliad*. Sarpedon was one of Zeus's sons by a mortal woman — so he was a mortal demigod not unlike Herakles or many others. When Zeus realized that Sarpedon, fighting for Troy, was about to be killed by Patroclus, fighting in the armor of

Achilles, he considered sweeping his son from the battlefield and dropping him back in his homeland in Lycia.

> *"...my Sarpedon, the man I love the most, my own son —*
> *doomed to die at the hands of Menoetius' son Patroclus.*
> *My heart is torn in two as I try to weigh all this.*
> *Shall I pluck him up, now, while he's still alive*
> *and set him down in the rich green land of Lycia,*
> *far from the war at Troy and all its tears?"*[33]

Hera reminded him that the other deathless gods had their own children engaged in the battle, and that if he whisked away his own son, he would set a precedent encouraging any of them to do so. If any god could snatch up one of their children at any time, the battle would become almost comically ridiculous, with heroes constantly disappearing in the midst of battle, whenever another fighter got the upper hand. Bravery and triumph would both be rendered meaningless without risk. Zeus agreed that his son would have to die to preserve order among the gods, but he "showered tears of blood that drenched the earth."

This is why I've said that the task of The Father is to contend with conceptual chaos. His struggle and conflict represents the process he has to go through, often privately, to determine the best course of action or policy. As a leader, The Father has to venture into dark realms of mystery and confusion that are avoided by others. He deals with this confusion of values and meaning and weighs potential outcomes of actions and precedents — so that they don't have to. If he is a benevolent Father, he is tormented by his sense of responsibility to others, knowing that poor choices — or simply, choices — may have negative effects on some of those who follow him, or for whose welfare he is ultimately responsible.

On a personal level, this involves looking inward and wrestling with your own problems and doing the dirty work of examining your own motivations and acknowledging weaknesses and tendencies that are destructive or out of sync with your stated mission or ideals.

This is an area in which meditation can be helpful. In most forms of meditation, you close your eyes and purposefully enter a state of darkness so that you can focus your mind's eye on ideas instead of objects. In this realm of pure concepts, it is possible to access the chaos of the unconscious — the more mysterious part of the mind — and possibly return with a new perspective, understanding, or inspiration. I like to think of this as "gathering kindling" for your own fire.

56

Odin's nocturnal self-sacrifice in the pursuit of knowledge gives us more insight into the spiritual ordeal of The Father in Darkness.

In the *Hávamál*, a collection of sayings in the *Poetic Edda* attributed to Odin, he recounts his choice to wound himself with a spear and hang from the world tree Yggdrasil for nine nights without food or drink, seeking some kind of revelation about the workings of the universe.

> *"I know that I hung*
> *on a windy tree*
> *for nine full nights*
> *wounded with a spear*
> *a sacrifice to Odin*
> *myself to myself*
> *on that tree*
> *which no man knows*
> *from what root it runs*

None made me happy with loaf
Or with horn
I looked down below
I took up the runes
Screaming I took them
And then fell down from there..."[34]

Odin falls down from the tree after discovering the runes, a Germanic system of writing in which the letters represent not only sounds, but also, as it believed by many, magical and elemental concepts which are hinted at in various rune poems. While this passage about Odin's tribulation has some surface similarities to Christ's crucifixion, Odin's motivation is not martyrdom or the cleansing of sin, but the pursuit of knowledge and understanding.

In another story, Odin transforms himself into a serpent so that he can sneak into a giant's mountain lair and seduce his daughter in order to steal the mead of poetry and inspiration to share with his fellow gods and men. During his escape, Odin transforms himself into an eagle — a trick and a form also associated with the Olympian Zeus. In this tale, The Father who reigns over man and the heavens above is again seen descending into a realm of darkness and taking on a darker form to obtain some enlightenment — some magic of the mind — and then returning to the sky triumphantly in the form of an eagle.

In a separate piece of lore, Odin also gives his eye to Mimir for a drink from his magical well of wisdom.

The struggle of The Father happens in darkness or seclusion or outside his domain, where the father must overcome a confusion of options or ideas. When enlightenment occurs, he returns to his realm of light to share his solution or new understanding.

In the case of the runes, Odin presents "the word." He delivers linguistic and magical technology. When Odin sacrifices his eye to Mimir for wisdom, he does so presumably to rule more effectively and solve the problems of his people. And when he steals the mead of poetry, he gives a form of verbal creativity and articulation to men and gods that makes life more joyful, more beautiful, and more interesting.

57

At the most atomic level and in the least complicated system, the father figure is a leader in both the practical and the spiritual sense. He is both king and high priest — or in the Platonic sense, a "philosopher king."

As groups become larger and more complex, the priesthood often becomes a separate, specialized role, but the king and the priesthood must work together harmoniously to ensure that kingship remains a sacred role. To maintain a sacred order, the leader-as-father must always be seen as an exemplary avatar of the idealized father above.

The figure of Odin is presumably a late variation on the Indo-European theme, but the mythology surrounding him recombines and reintegrates aspects of kingship and priesthood that were separated in other traditions and in more complex societies.

Loosely using Odin as a model, we can parse out some of the divisions within the roles of The Father and articulate different aspects of his character.

The Father as King in Darkness

The spear-wielding Odin represents The Father as warrior king and leader of the wild, bloodthirsty war band. In this aspect, he is the Roman Romulus — conqueror and creator of new orders.

He acts as a general or commander negotiating the conceptual chaos of battle, of choosing strategies and making life or death decisions.

The Father as King in Light

The Olympian Odin who presides over the world from his throne in a silver-roofed palace, and "rules in all matters,"[35] is more akin to a Roman Numa, the jurist king who oversees laws and establishes traditions and consistent order. He represents the role of the king as peacetime administrator. The King in Light delivers solutions and decisions after he has weighed the options and resolved his own confusion.

The Father as Priest in Darkness

When Odin ventures into darkness and confusion, or sacrifices "himself to himself" to seek some kind of answer or enlightenment, he is doing the darker work of the priest or magician. He is the wizard, delving into the hidden, the secret, and the unknown — King Arthur's Merlin. He is the priest as sacrificer, psychopomp, and shaman.

Odin also deals directly with spirits and the world of the dead, which is somewhat unusual for a sky god-king or father of gods. However, this characteristic makes Odin an exemplar for initiatory priests. Generally, initiation involves some sort of spiritual death and rebirth into a new social role. The initiated often become "the dead" or "the ancestors" and go out to the border zones beyond the perimeter of the town or city or what is perceived to be the ordered world — out into The Threshold — where they are subjected to some kind of ordeal which they must overcome before they can be reborn into their new role or identity. Odin's nine nights of suffering on the world tree are often regarded as a model for self-initiation in the pursuit of knowledge and self-transformation.

The Father as Priest in Light

The light aspects of The Father demonstrate the confident and benevolent administration of a solution. Valuations and meanings have already been decided or established, and The Father as Priest in Light oversees them according to doctrine. He celebrates and reaffirms sacred stories and valuations with the people and reminds them of sacred laws and hierarchies. The Father as Priest in Light is the "church father" or "god father." Odin can be seen as a Priest in Light in the Havamal, when he shares his wisdom and his advice with men.

58

The Father must go through darkness and confusion to create order, so all of these aspects of his nature are positive and productive. They are all part of his process, and The Father as King in Darkness as described here should not be confused with Jungian concepts like Moore's "Shadow King."

The Shadow King represents vulnerabilities or susceptibilities within the nature of the King archetype that may lead him to become bitchy or tyrannical. The King as Tyrant becomes corrupted by power and becomes addicted to the thrill of having and using power. Whereas the benevolent King theoretically uses power as a tool to do the greatest good for his people, the Tyrant king becomes exploitative and exercises his power for his own amusement and satisfaction. The Shadow King seeks power, not goodness or wisdom. The second type of Shadow King identified by Moore is what he calls the "Weakling" — the King who is insecure and paranoid and needs constant affirmation.

The Father in our system also includes the priest or "magician," and the Shadow of the wise man is the deceitful manipulator.

While these "shadow" aspects represent potential weaknesses in men, it is more important here to articulate the ideal, positive form of The Father — to describe what he is, instead of what he is not.

The popularization of psychology has created a widespread tendency to focus on sickness instead of health — to look for what is wrong instead of what is right.

A truly life-affirming philosophy, in the Nietzschean sense, must lead with and enshrine strength and health and the ideal.

59

We are, all of us, even the sun...products of the void. And, like the sun, one day we will burn out and return to the dark and directionless realm of everything and nothing. Chaos — that grand abyss beyond the scale of our imagining — is part of us, and we are part of it.

The creation of order, the work of The Father and of men, is a response to disorder and confusion and darkness. Just as the knight requires a dragon to slay or an enemy to fight in order to become what he is, The Father, the king, the creator of order requires mystery and disarray to become what he is and do what it is in his nature to do. To create hierarchy one must begin with some kind of anarchy.

In his emulation of The Father, man must descend into a realm of conceptual darkness, but to become and remain what he is, he must also return from it and continue to be an ordering source of illumination.

THE FATHER AS ASCENDED STRIKER

60

The Father creates his cosmos from chaos, but his roles as architect, surveyor, leader, and lawgiver cannot begin until the physical manifestations of chaos have been subdued or destroyed. Before he can build his kingdom, he must first seize possession of the realm and clear its perimeter of potential threats to his prospective order.

Odin could not make the earth or the trees or the mountains or the seas until he conspired with his brothers to murder the monstrous primeval being Ymir. Romulus and his brother had to kill Amulius, who had usurped their father's throne, before they could found the city of Rome. The brothers were themselves believed to be the descendants of Aeneas of Troy, who wandered the oceans before he landed in Italy and overcame Turnus, leader of some forces that rose against him, in battle. The Vedic Indra, who wields a thunderbolt weapon like Zeus, is the king of heaven, but he is most renown for killing the serpent Vrtra. And, in one of the oldest known cosmogonies, the Mesopotamian god Marduk ascended to his throne after he defeated the mother-monster Tiamat and, much like Odin, made the world of man from her corpse.

The repetition of this theme probably reflects the historical and practical habit of elevating a successful warrior or leader of warriors to a tribal leadership position. The men who have risked their lives to protect or conquer will obviously (and especially to each other) seem best qualified to lead other men who may be asked to do the same.

Zeus "who loves the lightning" is an ascended Striker who maintains the symbolism associated with warrior gods, even as father and king of the gods.

Zeus was the son of the Titan Cronus, of the first generation of gods brought forth by the primordial Sky Father, Uranus, who also begat the one-eyed Cyclopes and a race of monstrous hundred-handed giants. Uranus imprisoned the giants and the Cyclopes and installed the dragon Campe as their warden. Then Cronus and the other Titans rose up against their father, whom Cronus castrated. Cronus was viewed by the Greeks as a chaotic figure, who devoured all of his own children so that none of them could ever challenge his rule and overthrow him as he had overthrown his own father. His sister and consort Rhea deceived him to save her sixth son, Zeus, by feeding Cronus a stone and hiding Zeus in a cave, where he was fostered by nymphs (or possibly a goat). When Zeus came of age, he was able to induce his father to vomit up his brothers and sisters — who later became known as the Olympians —and together, they all went to war with their father Cronus and the other Titans. On the tenth year of that war, Zeus killed the dragon Campe and released the giants and Cyclopes. The Cyclopes forged him his thunderbolt, and also gave a helmet to Pluto and a trident to Poseidon. Thus armed and allied with the hundred-handers and the Cyclopes, the Olympians were finally able to defeat Cronus and the Titans and imprison them in Tartarus.

While the story about the dragon Campe comes only from the late *Library of (Pseudo) Apollodorus*, in both his *Library* and

Hesiod's *Theogony*, Zeus was forced to battle the terrible beast Typhon before he could take command of his kingdom. Typhon was borne of the earth mother Gaia, and "a hundred fearsome snake-heads" sprung from his shoulders.

> "...when Zeus had raised up his might and seized his arms, thunder and lightning and lurid thunderbolt, he leaped from Olympus and struck him, and burned all the marvellous heads of the monster about him. But when Zeus had conquered him and lashed him with strokes, Typhon was hurled down, a maimed wreck, so that the huge earth groaned."[36]

With the war over and Typhon defeated, the warrior Zeus ascended to become the king of the heavens, who ruled over the Olympian gods and men from his mountain realm above. His brother Poseidon was given dominion over the seas and his brother Pluto was allotted rule over Hades, realm of the dead. Zeus ruled with his sister and consort Hera, but he fathered the next generation of gods — Apollo, Athena, Artemis, Aphrodite, Hermes, Dionysus and Hephaestus — as well as numerous demigods, by numerous women and sometimes, as with Athena, by sheer will alone.

61

In the Greek lore, Cronus is the paranoid Shadow Tyrant who castrates his father and eats his own children to keep them from growing, certain that they will surpass him. Zeus was raised in foster care — a theme often repeated in stories about heroes and future kings — until he was old enough to free his brothers and sisters and make war on his tyrannical father and the Titans. Like the prototypical hero, he must kill a dragon or serpent as part of his overcoming and becoming. He commands thunder and lightning like Thor and wields a thunderbolt that, in early depictions, resembles Indra's vajra.

Zeus demonstrated that he was able to overcome physical chaos before he took on the work of contending with the conceptual chaos of ruling, rule-making, and valuation.

After he ascended to his throne, although he was known to thunder about in the heavens and toss the occasional authoritative bolt, the duties of war-making and dragon-slaying were also passed on to others — like his son Apollo, who killed the chthonic serpent Python, and his son Herakles, who slew the Lernaean Hydra. Metaphorically speaking, his strikers and heroes become his bolts of lightning, sent out to strike down forces of chaos and impose his righteous order on his behalf.

SYMBOLS OF THE GUARDIANS

62

In Plato's system, the counselors are selected from among the auxiliary — the warrior class — and the two groups work symbiotically to form a combined "guardian" class. In many of the mythological systems discussed here, the king begins as a warrior, or slays a beast that represents chaos. As the roles of warrior and patriarch often overlap or demonstrate a transition from one role to another, the symbolism and the symbolic weapons and the items associated with the king or "allfather" have tended to overlap with the symbols and symbolic weapons associated with the warrior class. The warriors represent the power of the king and the king is either an ascended warrior or his power comes from being commander-in-chief of military forces. Along with solar symbols and allusions to the sky, the combined symbolism of the guardians generally includes tools used to hunt and fight — to impose will and therefore impose order on chaos both conceptually and physically. As Veblen observed in *The Theory of the Leisure Class*, the heraldric and status symbols associated with the noble classes have long tended to invoke "rapacious beasts" and "birds of prey" and tools of violence. [37] While, like modern sports teams, the great and commanding houses of old represented themselves with images of lions and tigers and bears and the occasional dragon — all emblematic of strength and ferocity and employed to invoke fear — the highest ideal is necessarily located in the sky, so the symbolism of the idealized guardian class of gods and exemplars most often and most logically evokes an upward glance. From our earthbound station, men looked upward to the sun, to the strike of lightning, to soaring birds of prey — and they imagined shining celestial versions of their own battle chariots racing across the sky.

63

The Sun

The sun is the highest symbol of the guardian class — it halos The Father and shines down on his golden warriors and heroes. The sun is often seen as "the eye of the father" throughout various Indo-European religions.

The sun has been discussed throughout this book so there is no reason to elaborate on its symbolic centrality again here. However, I'll add a few notes about the lightning and the thunderbolts, the birds of prey, the bulls, and the chariots that have been associated with the heavenly guardians again and again.

The Thunderbolt

In some mythical systems, the father wields thunder and lightning, as with ascended warrior god-kings like Zeus and Indra, and in others, the storm weapons of thunder and lightning are operated by the secondary function striker gods like Thor. A commonality is lightning or the "thunderbolt" imagined as the ultimate weapon of god.

One can imagine how spectacular and otherworldly lightning must have seemed to primitive men — and how seeing it strike down a sturdy oak with a single, decisive blow must have seemed like the supernatural equivalent of strikes with fists and early weapons. Likewise, perhaps in part because the oak is a natural lightning rod — connecting it in some way to the heavens — it has long been recognized as an earthbound symbol of the divine strength of patriarchs, kings, and warriors.

Trying to imagine what the thunder and lightning weapon of the sky father or the sky warrior looked like must have been somewhat challenging. It has been portrayed as an axe, a spear, or a double spindle whose Greek name was *keraunos*. Occasionally, the thunderbolt weapon was envisioned as a kind of "double-pronged lightning fork" that resembled a tuning fork. Further East, the hand-held double bolt took on an almost lotus-like form as Indra's vajra. In some representations, Zeus is pictured holding a very similar object. In the North, Thor's hammer Mjolnir became the iconic thunder weapon.[38]

The weapon of a god or ideal is a means of symbolizing his violent power and his ability to impose his will and maintain his order. In the hand of The Father, one could envision that power being used in a spiritual realm of ideas and forms to do battle with and overcome conceptual threats to his order — wielding it, to borrow and repurpose the words of Heraclitus, "to steer all things." [39] In the hand of The Striker, it is a physical weapon, employed to strike down physical threats to survival, to the survival of the order, and to the continuation of the fire.

The Sceptre

Zeus and Jupiter were often shown holding a sceptre with a bird on it to show their authority, and ceremonial scepters of rule have been held by emperors and kings and leaders in Europe, the Middle East, and northern Africa from antiquity to modern times. The sceptre may be a refinement of the tribal "talking stick," or it may in some cases symbolically represent the *axis mundi* itself — because the king or The Father is connected to the sacred axis of the world, and all rules and lines of differentiation and valuation emanate from his center.

A scepter would not be associated with warriors, and would be exclusive to The Father — the priest or the king.

Eagles and Birds of Prey

In his daylight incarnation, the solar king Ra was depicted as a falcon, a raptor similar to the eagle.

Zeus was known to take the form of an eagle during his sexual adventuring on earth, and he frequently sent eagles down as omens. For instance, when Odysseus's young son invoked the thunder king's name in a wish for his father to have vengeance on his mother's opportunistic suiters, "farseeing Zeus sent down a sign" and two eagles descended from a mountain and tore each other apart above the crowd of men. [40] Elsewhere in the story, Zeus' eagles murder fat geese in a dream and one is seen "clutching a trembling dove."[41]

Odin transformed himself into an eagle when he stole the mead of poetry from the giant Suttungr, and in *The Rig Veda*, it is an eagle who brings Indra the mysterious "soma" drink that makes men "ecstatic."

> "Oh Maruts, the bird shall be supreme above all birds, the swift-flying eagle above all eagles, since by his own driving power that needs no chariot wheels, with his powerful wings he brought to man the oblation loved by the gods."[42]

The eagle shares the sky with the sun, in the realm of The Father. The predatory eagle dives down from the sky with speed and divine precision to prey on the creatures of the earth and the water, but resides high above in tree and mountaintop aeries, far out of reach. The powerful eagle who sees and judges the world from high above is a natural and obvious choice to represent the high and all-seeing Father. And as representatives of The Father who strike down from above like lightning, they are also logical symbols to associate with The Striker.

As avian omens, they carry messages from the gods, and in the cases of the mead of poetry and soma — the exhilarating drink that inspires men to speak — eagles both deliver and bless the sacred drink that men and gods share together in spirit.

It is notable that Odin, so often presented in mystery and darkness and associated with death and wisdom, is more normally pictured with his ravens, Huginn and Muninn ("thought" and "memory"). Ravens are imposing and intelligent birds, but more often scavengers than predators, and in the North they were known, like wolves, for feasting on the corpses of the dead left on the battlefield. Perhaps the raven is the most appropriate feathered representative of The Father in Darkness.

The Chariot

Anyone who has worked a piece of land or even gone to the grocery store understands what a game-changer a cart with wheels must have been to our ancient ancestors. But sky gods rarely ride in carts. Gods of the earth and the harvest, like Freyr, are sometimes described as having wagons. Sky gods — kings and warriors — ride in golden horse-drawn wagons of war. They ride in chariots.

An epithet of Indra was rathe ṣṭhā, which corresponds to the Iranian raθaēštā, literally: "in chariot standing, i.e. charioteer." In the words of Émile Benveniste, "This descriptive term goes back to the heroic age with its idealization of the warrior and its celebration of the young fighter who, standing upright in his chariot, hurls himself into the fray."[43]

According to anthropologist David W. Anthony in his book *The Horse, The Wheel and Language*, war chariots were invented around 2100 BC in the Eurasian steppes during the period in which Indo-European languages and cultures were developing and spreading. They were effective in tribal wars in the steppes because they were "noisy, fast and intimidating, and provided an elevated platform from which a skilled driver could hurl a sheath full of javelins."[44] They were the terrifying war machines of invading and conquering forces. Maneuvering them took great skill and a lot of practice, indicating the emergence of a specialized class of dedicated warriors, which itself was also a sign of a wealthy and prosperous people living well beyond mere subsistence. Like a weapon, in myth the chariot was a symbol of esteem and of power and it represented the means by which a group of men imposed and maintained their order and identity. And, much like the sword, chariots remained symbolic of martial power long after men ceased using them as their primary weapons of war. Chariot races continued and were featured at the Olympic Games, at Roman gladiatorial games and remained popular as a sport for exhibition and entertainment well into the Christian era.

In myth, chariots were often imagined as the vehicles of the sun itself — replacing the Egyptian barge and other means of transportation. In *The Rig Veda*, Sūrya the personification of the sun — also referred to as "the eye of Varuna"— drives across the sky in a chariot pulled by seven mares. Indra and his Maruts ride chariots into battle. The Sumerian god Utu, later worshipped by the Akkadians, Assyrians, and Babylonians as Shamash, was another sun god who rode a chariot across the sky and oversaw all things. The Greek god of the sun Helios rides in a chariot, and the elegant solar hero Apollo took flight in a golden chariot pulled by swans. Chariots carried Homer's fighting men and demigods at the battle of Troy, and the competitive chariot race is first described during the funeral games of Patroclus. The Trundholm Sun Chariot provides evidence that the story of the sun chariot reached bronze age Scandinavia, where the sun was described as a goddess, although this is possibly a consequence of the re-gendering of the sun as a feminine noun in Germanic languages. Chariot battles are found even in the old Irish epic, the *Táin Bó Cúailnge*, though there is little or no evidence of chariots having been used for battle in Ireland. Rather, the chariot is likely a continuation of an older, more mythic theme in which glorious, high status warriors hurl spears from terrible but beautiful chariots driven by "trusty sidekick" charioteers, as with Cú Chulainn and Láeg.

Today, the chariot itself is an anachronism — though little more anachronistic than the spear or the bow or even the horse. However, men are still known to refer to their mechanical rides figuratively as steeds and chariots, and many still measure their ability to carry a vehicle's weight at speed in "horsepower." The chariot drives through history and the ages of heroes as a symbol of the power of the men who fought for dominance over other men and the power of the kings and leaders who commanded them. And, in the context of this integrated mythopoetic system, they have also become — at Plato's suggestion — the horse-drawn war carts that carry our souls.

The Bull

The people who spoke Proto-Indo-European, from whom we've inherited so many of these myths, were a "male-centered" and "cattle-raising" people.[45] Cattle were highly valuable, but were also more difficult to steal and herd away than stationary crops. The importance of cattle to the lives of pastoral eurasians was reflected in their myths and the myths that developed from them.

Indra and his war band, the Maruts, are all referred to repeatedly as bulls in *The Rig Veda*. Bulls figure prominently in the art of ancient Crete, and in early cults there, Zeus may have been represented as a bull. Zeus took the form of a bull in some of his exploits, and heroes like Herakles, Theseus and Jason were all tasked with contending with wild and unruly bulls. Bulls were sacrificed to please Apollo and Zeus and his brother Poseidon in the works of Homer, and both gods and warriors were compared to powerful bulls in *Iliad*. Oxen — castrated bulls used as draft animals — were also frequently traded and given as gifts to men and slaughtered in the name of the gods.[46] The Vedic Mitra and the Iranian Mithra was Hellenized and resurrected during the Roman Empire in the underground cults of Mithras — a solar warrior god who was shown overcoming and slaughtering a bull.[47]

There is a theme of cattle-raiding and the rescuing of cattle that runs from *The Rig Veda* to the Irish epic known as "The Cattle Raid of Cooley" or the *Táin Bó Cúailnge*. In *The Rig Veda*, cows are symbolically referred to almost interchangeably with both wealth and water, and Indra is praised for finding the cows and releasing them from a cave. Herakles was tasked with fetching the cattle of Geryon, and Odysseus is punished by Zeus when his hungry men killed the cattle of Helios, god of the sun. The god Hermes, invoked as a cattle rustler, mischievously steals Apollo's cattle in *The Homeric Hymns*. The entire plot of the *Táin Bó Cúailnge* revolves around the theft of a massive stud bull, Donn Cuailnge, who could "bull fifty heifers every day," was so large that, "his shadow could shelter a hundred warriors from heat or cold," and who eventually gored the only bull who could compete with him in an epic bovine battle.

The hunting of bulls and cattle reaches back to prehistory and the wild ancestors of cattle, now extinct, like the giant European aurochs depicted in cave paintings and symbolized by the Anglo-Saxon rune Ur. It stood almost 6 feet tall at the shoulder, and its rune poem describes it as being proud and savage and fighting with its horns —"a creature of great mettle."[48]

The worlds of these myths may seem distant and unfamiliar, but cattle rustling and horse thieving were a challenge for men on the American frontier not so very long ago at all. With wide open territories and grazing assets, the "Old West" was a lot like the *very* old West. American and Mexican ranchers struggled with cattle theft from competitors and Native American tribes, and the cattle raid was used as a tactic by the Confederate army in the Civil War. The men who herded and managed cattle were forced to develop a set of skills that would have been familiar to men in Vedic India or Ancient Greece, and these "cowboys" demonstrated their courage, grit, and prowess to each other by riding bulls — still practiced as a sport at rodeos today.

Bulls are symbols of virile power and dominance. They are a powerful physical monster that our distant ancestors and frontier cowboys and even some men today have had to contend with and overcome. They are dangerous and can be aggressive and territorial — much like men. As such, they came to represent masculine triumph, courage, and strength. At the same time they are assets, symbols of status and wealth and power. The most easily recognizable rendering of a bull today is probably the Wall Street Bull, which has become a symbol of rising stock prices.

64

Scanning through the symbols commonly associated with warriors, kings, fathers, and leaders could no doubt produce a wider collection of symbols. This handful of symbols that, but for the sceptre, seem to be collective symbols of the "guardian" class is merely a starting point. The sun, the thunderbolt, the bird of prey, the bull — these are dominant symbols that have been repeatedly associated with rulers and their champions throughout not only Indo-European cultures but also Mesopotamian and no doubt many other cultures.

"The thunderbolt steers all things."

— Heraclitus

THE STRIKER

Champion of Order

65

The Striker is characterized by the weapon, the tool which is an extension of his own nature. The Striker represents man himself as a weapon, a tool for creating, maintaining, and expanding the perimeter of sacred order.

The Father wields the weapon. The Striker *is* the weapon. The Striker is heaven's storm. He is the lightning and the wind and the rolling thunder.

No order can be created without violent force, employed against the physical forces of chaos that threaten to dissolve order and return man to a void without meaning, orientation, or any hierarchy of values — whether in death or in some perilous and utterly confused state of existence. The universe itself is chaotic and uncertain to man, and he must do war with it to create and maintain even some semblance of order and certainty, however transient that state of order and ultimately futile that war may be. It is only in these pockets of order and certainty that man is able to thrive and perpetuate his own existence.

To suggest that the violence of man is employed *only* to *protect* or *defend* order is a charming philosophical pleasantry — a just-so story to shelter women and children from the brutal truth that masculine violence is offensive as well as defensive. For the order of man to expand beyond the light of a single campfire, it must be directed outward to impose that order on an ever greater territory. The creation of order is inherently aggressive. The strike in response is a tactically inferior position to the pre-emptive or ambitious strike. This is why The Striker is more fully and properly understood as a champion of order, and not merely its defender. Order must not only be protected — it must also be imposed — and the order that is imposed must then be protected.

66

The Striker, as a god or perfected ideal, is the Platonic form of a warrior. He is not any one warrior, but what we mean when we say warrior. The Striker is the eternal spirit of the warrior and the weapon — superhuman and beyond reach. As The Father is the father-beyond-fathers, The Striker is the warrior-beyond-warriors.

The Striker is a combination of qualities and a paragon of virtues. Men anthropomorphize these abstract adjectives into a proper noun so that they can better imagine what is beyond imagination. Given shape and character, he takes on the aspects of Indra, the young Zeus and Marduk, Apollo, Mars, and Thor.

To humanize these ethereal gods by another degree, men — especially the Greeks — created demigod Strikers. Sons of gods and goddesses like Herakles and Theseus and Achilles and Aeneas were believed to have walked the earth as mortal men and performed heroic deeds and fought in great wars.

When reading ancient stories, it is impossible in many cases to know which demigods were great men whose stories were embellished, and which god-like men were entirely invented by poets and storytellers. Even when men's deeds are meticulously documented, we can see widely admired men take on a mythic quality and we can observe a kind of implicit apotheosis in the popular imagination after their deaths. If we discovered that Herakles was just a strong guy who became the subject of tall tales, would that be more inspiring? Or would the stories about him be more inspiring if we knew for certain he had never existed at all? How much does it matter? Men are inspired by true stories as well as fiction. What matters is the sway that the stories exert over our imaginations and our unconscious mind.

Purists may balk, but I often include well-known superheroes and movie characters in discussions about men and Strikers because they represent the same ideas — and they are alive and powerful in the minds of millions of men.

The Striker is an ideal form, but the ideal endures in our mental and spiritual universes because The Striker represents qualities that continue to be evident in real men in the real world. We've all met or heard about men in our own lifetimes who seem to embody the Striker qualities. These are the kind of men who have excelled in real combat or the ritualized and symbolic combat of sport, or men who have risked their lives for others or even for glory, or men who always seem to be preparing to do *that thing* and be *that guy* if necessary.

The Striker has many names, but when universalized and integrated and recognized as an eternal form — has there ever been a god more actively and passionately revered, a god more practically emulated by more men?

For thousands and thousands of years, likely long before we were even homo sapiens — wide-eyed with simian awe — countless generations of boys and men have looked up to and wanted to be more like the men in their midst who were mighty and gallant.

Even today, their thumbs tap away as they affirmatively and enthusiastically "like" videos and images of men who hunt and fight, who perform feats of strength and daring and tactical virtuosity, who exude an aura of dominant confidence. The Striker is who they play in video games and who they want to see in movies and the man who they want to read about in books. The Striker is the idealized version of a man who is very good at being a man. There is a part of every man who wants to be valued as a man among men, so The Striker is an idealized version of each and all men. The Striker represents pure, idealized masculinity.

67

The name "The Striker" is the rough English equivalent of what is believed to be the earliest Indo-European name of the god who champions order in the name of The Father. Linguists and comparative mythologists have reconstructed the name *perkʷunos for the thundering warrior god of the Proto-Indo-Europeans, based on surviving evidence in other languages and a proposed *PIE root, *per-, which meant "to strike" and/or was associated with the oak tree (*pérkʷus). Lightning tends to strike oaks more frequently than other trees, and the two concepts have been associated for a very long time.

The closest god names to Perkwunos come from the Baltic and Slavic regions. The Lithuanians, who were the last European pagans to convert to Christianity in the Fifteenth Century, called their thundering warrior god of the storms Perkūnas. The Latvians called the same god Pērkons. According to comparative mythologist Jaan Puhvel, Russian folklore "has much to tell of Perún," who slew a serpent on a mountain to release cattle and water, like the Vedic god Indra, and who produced "thunder and fiery slivers of rock."[49]

68

In Indo-European lore, physical chaos has most often been represented by some kind of serpent. The snake is, symbolically, the antithesis of the eagle. While the eagle hovers above boldly and in plain sight, the serpent is low to the ground and shelters in shadows. Both raptors and vipers are strikers, but one comes down from above in the light of the sun, and the other is a danger that lurks in the unknown — a mysterious, chthonic threat that poisons before it devours. The serpent has often been associated with mystery cults, with the occult, and with women.

In the North, the words for dragons and snakes, like the Old English *wyrm* and the Old Norse *ormr*, also refer to worms and may come from a Proto-Indo-European root that means "to turn" as snakes twist and worms turn the earth. The worm is a reminder of death and our inevitable return to the earth and the undifferentiated abyss. The worm evokes the cycle of life and the connectedness of all things, and this has been captured in the symbol of the circular snake that devours even itself — the ouroboros — depicted in an ancient alchemical document with the motto "the all is one."

The ouroboros is repeated in northern mythology as Jörmungandr, the world serpent and mortal foe of the striking god Thor. This giant, venomous serpent resides in the ocean and wraps around the entire world of man, enclosing it, reminiscent of Indra's serpentine enemy Vṛtra who withholds the waters. The Striker does battle with the serpent to stave off death and make vital existence possible, but like Thor, he and all of us must succumb to it in the end.

One of the oldest repeated poetic expressions has been rendered in Proto-Indo-European as "(h_1e) g^wént $h_1$óg^{w}im," meaning, "He killed the serpent."[50]

This one phrase encapsulates the eternal role of The Striker and of man as striker — to do battle with and overcome the forces of physical chaos. It was recently repeated succinctly in a book of observations about men written by a modern warrior, Michael Kurcina, titled "We Fight Monsters."[51]

While the monsters that Striker gods battled were most often serpents and dragons and grotesque combinations of snakes with other animals, Strikers also fought a bestiary of other imaginative creatures. Each archetypal juxtaposition evokes its own meaning, as with Theseus and the Minotaur — a man-eating abomination who was part man and part bull, a punishment of shame, cuckery, and bestiality sent by Poseidon in response to a promise broken by King Minos. The labyrinth constructed to hide the shame of that beastly bastard created another level of symbolic meaning.

In the North, Strikers like Thor most often fought jötnar, creatures commonly called "giants," but whose name actually meant something like "devourers." They were not always physically large, and sometimes they were attractive. Still, they symbolized a dehumanized "other" — a stand-in for a human enemy or outsider who threatened from beyond the protected enclosure. Much like a jötunn, Grendel, the monster who *Beowulf* killed, was an unnaturally large and possibly deformed man-eating humanoid. And his mother was even worse.

Sometimes, the monsters have merely been other men — the monsters among us and most like us. Before Theseus volunteered to fight the Minotaur, as a young man, he took a journey during which he killed a handful of men who are often described as bandits. However, in contemporary terms, most would be called "serial killers."

One of them lured wayward travelers over to help him with some trees he was bending, then released his grip, and his victims were either torn apart or shot into the air. Another killer forced passersby to wash his feet and then kicked them off a cliff. One creep named Procrustes offered folks a bed to sleep in, and then fit them into it perfectly by sadistically sawing off their limbs or stretching them to death. The early adventures of Theseus could easily be reworked into a modern horror movie.

Theseus is best known for killing the Minotaur, but he started out killing bad men. This is The Striker in his most accessible, relatable form — as a strong, courageous, and capable man who sees something disordered and evil, and decides to take it upon himself to correct that evil to save innocent people from cruelty, suffering, and death. While the psychopath kills for the sake of killing, The Striker, in his noblest manifestation, kills to save life.

A Striker is a man of action, and we remember him for his actions — he is identified most often not only for his abilities, but for what he did and which monsters he killed. A Striker is defined by his monsters and his feats are valued according to the ferocity of his opponents. The greater the monster, the greater the man.

Men through the ages have certainly been challenged to hunt and fight monstrous natural creatures that threaten chaos to their worlds — whether beastly apex predators like lions, bears, and packs of wolves or man-goring prey like wild boars and horned bulls. Yet, in most cases, it is other men who will make the most dangerous game. The beasts of myth, however supernatural or fantastical, can symbolize the complex challenges that men face in contending with the chaos created for men by other men, albeit in a dehumanized and metaphorical way.

69

The virtues of The Striker are the virtues required to "fight monsters" at the edge of the perimeter and beyond. They are the primal and primary virtues required of men, and which men have always required of each other, to hunt and to fight and to overcome the forces of physical chaos that may threaten their survival, the survival of their friends and loved ones, and the survival of their orders. The virtues of The Striker are the virtues universally associated with masculinity — the "tactical virtues" of Strength, Courage, Mastery, and Honor that I explained at length in *The Way of Men*.

If you ignited a fire with a group of men in the open wilderness, Strength, Courage, Mastery, and Honor are the virtues that the men in your group would need and value and look for in each other as they faced outward into the darkness and prepared to engage whatever went bump in the night, whatever animated terrors lurked just beyond their sight — man or animal.

The root of the word virtue itself is *vir*, the Latin word meaning both man and warrior, which comes from the Proto-Indo-European **wiHrós*, whose own root **weyh₁-* means "to hunt." And, in all of its variations from the Sanskrit वीर (*vīrá*) to the Old Norse *verr* and the Old English *wer*, this word means both man and warrior or hero. To have *virtue* in the ancient world meant to have the qualities, first, of a man — the attributes of a hunter and fighter and a hero, a champion of order.

Thor is familiar to almost all modern readers because of the Marvel comic book movies. While those films don't always represent the documented mythic details of the thunderer from the North very well, his character and his primary virtues have, for the most part, remained intact. Thor is known for his strength and his courage, his skill in fighting, his loyalty, and his service to right order. Like Captain America, another Striker, he's a straight arrow. The essence of The Striker is the young, confident warrior. If fate allows, he matures into a more complex man, but that is a development of his nature and not its primal core.

The tactical virtues of The Striker are prominent in all of the labors of Herakles. Zeus' son was known first for his strength —he wrestled the Nemean Lion and captured the Cretan bull. Overcoming fear of death, he ventured into the world of the dead to defeat the three-headed dog that guarded its entrance, and drag him back to the world of the living. Each of his assigned labors required more than courage and brute force. He was forced to use his head — to be a problem solver. After realizing that the Lernaean Hydra grew two new heads for every one that he cut off, he enlisted the help of his nephew, Iolaus, to use a firebrand to cauterize the wounds — preventing new growth. Herakles also diverted a river to clean the stables of 3,000 cattle in a single day.

Herakles undertook his famous labors to redeem his reputation in the eyes of gods and men — and probably so that he could look at his own reflection in the mirror. Driven mad by Hera, he had slain his whole family, and he performed his labors for King Eurystheus to attempt to restore his honor.

70

Xenophon, a student of Socrates and warrior in his own right, retold a story about young Herakles in his *Memorabilia* that became a favorite theme among Greek, Roman, and Renaissance writers and artists. It is sometimes referred to as "Herakles at the crossroads." When Herakles was coming of age and becoming independent, he sat down to ponder his direction. He was visited by virtue and vice, personified as two female spirits named Areté and Kakia.

Kakia was a fat, painted tramp who called herself "happiness," but admitted that others called her vice. She offered Herakles a life without responsibility, in which he would only need concern himself with selecting whichever food and drink and sexual company he preferred. He would not have to work, merely consume and enjoy whatever luxuries appealed to him.

Areté, on the other hand, was dressed conservatively and appeared to be extremely dignified. She offered a far harder, but nobler path, saying:

> "*Nothing that is really good and admirable is granted by the gods to men without some effort and application. If you want the gods to be gracious to you, you must worship the gods; if you wish to be loved by your friends, you must be kind to your friends; if you desire to be honoured by a State, you must help that State; if you expect to be admired for your fine qualities by the whole of Greece, you must try to benefit Greece; if you want your land to produce abundant crops, you must look after your land; if you expect to make money from your livestock, you must take care of your livestock; if you have an impulse to extend your influence by war, and want to be able to free your friends and subdue your enemies, you must both learn the actual arts of war from those who understand them, and practice the proper way of applying them; and if you want to be physically efficient, you must train your body to be subject to your reason, and develop it with hard work and sweat.*"[52]

Areté translates roughly to "excellence," and as described above, represents a commitment to an independent mastery of the manly arts and, more broadly, to all things. Vice represented a life that is essentially dependent on some external source. Excellence is a value that creates hierarchy and is favored by the figure of The Father and his order. Areté offered Herakles a choice between a path that assists in the creation and maintenance of order, a life on the perimeter where men are tested, or a safe and pleasant life of illusion within the perimeter, where men are cared for and entertained like children. Vice offered the disordered state of the Lord of the Earth, where appetites are indulged to the extreme.

Of course, Herakles, as a hero and son of Zeus, chose the path of excellence.

71

The primary function of The Striker is to contend with physical chaos. Characterized by thumos, he uses physical force to put the world in order, and to maintain that order.

To become what he is, The Striker must take and remain on a path of areté. But what characterizes him emotionally is the spur of thumos.

Thumos is probably best understood as righteous indignation. The man animated by thumos takes responsibility for justice personally. He says, "this injustice cannot stand, and if no one will stand up for what is right, then I will." The Striker is the exemplar of manly virtue, and as political philosopher Harvey Mansfield observed in his book on manliness, while all people experience thumotic feelings, those whom we regard as particularly manly are thumotic "in excess."[53] The thumotic man doggedly defends his own, and in a more abstract sense, his own order against what he recognizes to be a threat of chaos. It is "the doggish part of the human soul" that "defends human ends higher than itself," and by defending the value of what is higher — his sacred order — asserts his belief in the inherent worth of that order.[54] The Striker defends what he believes to be the work of The Father, and as its champion he is absolutely necessary for the creation, enforcement and expansion of any ordered world. He sees something that he believes to be wrong, and he takes it upon himself to become the weapon of The Father and right that wrong.

Returning to our chariot, thumos is not the charioteer — he is one of the horses. He is the horse of noble origin, a steed of the sky, but he is still a wild beast who must be guided and reined.

Loyal as he is to order, when not guided by wisdom and a righteous Father, he can be too easily whipped down a dark road.

He is a horse that wants to run and a dog that wants to fight. To become what he is and realize his potential — and in the absence of clear and undeniable threats to his own and the good around him, he can sometimes be too easily convinced by a clever and self-serving charioteer.

I have known many extremely thumotic men, and they are exactly the kind of men you want to have around in an emergency, and they embody and truly want to be everything good and right about men. But it is in their natures, especially when they are very young, to be a touch innocent and naive. They are sometimes too easily manipulated by men who I call "the organ grinders of thumos," after the old street musicians who played songs and trained monkeys to dance to them. These "organ grinders" play angry songs that tap into the part of men that wants to get angry and be angry and stay angry — the part that wants to fight first and ask questions later.

That righteous, thumotic anger can become an addiction. I've experienced it myself, as many men have, especially in this age of news and propaganda. It becomes a habit to wake up in the morning and seek out the narrative that makes you angry and see the whole world in red. Some surrogate father who produces this kind of narrative — who plays this angry tune — can too easily convince us to go out and fight for his own profit or aggrandizement, while making it seem like we are defending what is good and right. In a simple society, there is only one father-leader and one order to champion. In this more complicated, confusing, and far more cosmopolitan society, there are many organ grinders and would-be charioteers. Any number of seductively smooth-talking Emperor Palpatines will stoke your anger and send you to your doom for their own gain or for the rush of power alone. So my advice to young thumotic men is to be very careful, remember what is truly important to you at your core — what has always been important to you — and if you're going to go to battle, choose your charioteer wisely.

Make sure the man who you follow values your life and your honor. Don't settle for a cheap organ grinder who just wants to make his monkeys dance.

Thumos spurs a man not only to stand up for others and what is right, but also for himself. And in this, too, it can be good or evil. A man who won't stand up for himself or assert his interests, and who won't take the challenge to better himself will never be well-regarded by men as a man. This spirit makes a man demand to be respected and makes him want to be honored among men.

And if he feels that he has been disrespected or unfairly dishonored, this thumos can turn into an all-consuming rage. The *Iliad* begins, "Sing, O muse, of the rage of Achilles..."

This rage can drive men to glory. Men often achieve a great deal in angered response to some real or perceived slight or sense that they have been underrated or treated unjustly. It is common in the age of therapeutic age to reduce or dismiss such a man's accomplishments by pointing this out, but in so doing, they reveal in themselves the mindset of an overprotective mother or a jealous and less accomplished man. I do not believe that a man's achievements mean less because "he had something to prove." Thumotic rage is a powerful motivator and a legitimate starting point. Gyms are full of young men listening to angry music, pushing themselves in defiant response to some sense that they are or are expected to be less than they believe they could become. As they prove themselves and become more confident, however, it is healthier to move beyond rage as a primary motivator and begin to achieve as a form of self-love or to strive in the service of excellence itself. Too much rage, nurtured for too long, can become poisonous and destructive to the man himself, and often leads to pointless and unhinged recklessness.

Ares, the Greek god of war, was acknowledged as the manliest of gods and revered by the Spartans, but the moderate Athenians were wary of him, and he was sometimes depicted as a bit of a buffoon. They associated him with bloodlust and violence for its own sake, having no doubt seen how that force can take possession of a man's soul.

In a hymn to Ares, invoked as "King of Manliness," the Greeks asked the god to:

> *"Shed down a kindly ray from above upon my life, and strength of war, that I may be able to drive away bitter cowardice from my head and crush down the deceitful impulses of my soul.*
> *Restrain also the keen fury of my heart which provokes me to tread the ways of blood-curdling strife.*
> *Rather, O blessed one, give me boldness to abide within the harmless laws of peace, avoiding strife and hatred and the violent fiends of death."*[55]

When the mythos of Ares was eventually syncretized with that of the already extant Roman god Mars, the exemplar of manly warriors was rendered more purposefully and given more weight. The spear of Mars was still terrifying to call, as King Latinus refused to in *The Aeneid*[56] — but also revered as an indispensable champion of order and even, like his counterpart Thor, as a protector of crops. The Romans saw the warrior god as a protector of peace and prosperity, a perspective that brings to mind the very Roman adage, *Si vis pacem, para bellum.* (If you want peace, prepare for war.)

72

The Striker, animated by the wild and potentially deadly spirit of thumos and charged with battling physical chaos, has his own form of darkness to contend with, and I'll explore that further in the next chapter. However, he is not that darkness. He is the weapon of light that responds to it.

Viewed as an exemplar, as a proud and noble eagle, in his purest form he is the righteous champion of order who makes the world within the perimeter safe and makes all other forms of prosperity possible.

There is certainly a wiser, more mature, more experienced, a little more measured and world-weary manifestation of The Striker, perhaps best developed in older characters like Odysseus — who in his story had also already been a father and a king. There have always been grizzled warriors who truly know what it is to be a Striker, and only they can describe that experience with any authenticity.

From talking to a few, I've gotten the sense that the pure ideal of The Striker is still alive in a lot of them, and when they're called to do that bloody work, they brush aside any cynicism and tap into the spirit that started them down that path, even when they have settled on the idea that they are merely guns for hire.

It is young men who are initiated into battle and it is young men who have fought the majority of wars. The perfect, undefiled kernel of the Striker's spirit is the spirit of a thumotic young man going out into the fray for the first time, or enlisting in the military or the police because he believes in a just cause. He feels that he is needed, and goes to find glory or death because he truly believes that he is doing right, that he is doing good, and fighting evil — whether historians after the fact, who always have access to more information than he had at that moment, determine that he was right or wrong.

We can naturally call upon myth or the epics to depict this, but in my own lifetime I have known many men who volunteered to join the military after 9/11, because they truly believed that they were protecting their loved ones, protecting the only order they had ever known and fighting the forces of chaos and evil. That is what The Striker is, and what he does, and those men were possessed by the spirit of The Striker. They experienced thumos, and took action. And, for our purposes here, it doesn't matter if, in the final analysis, we believe that they were right or wrong.

73

Most of us will never be forced to defend our order or our loved ones, and most men will never go to war. That has been the case for a very long time. The majority of men have worked farms or been craftsmen or traders. George Washington was also a surveyor and a farmer. He spent some of his life in war, some of it as a leader, and a lot of it as a man performing the work that perpetuates life. But thumos, the desire to be seen as a man of worth, and a man among men, the desire to demonstrate the tactical virtues of Strength, Courage, Mastery, and Honor — these are all essential parts of all men who are worthy of that designation.

Opportunities to demonstrate these virtues won't always be found in the glory of battle. They may be less dramatic, and our confrontations may not be "life or death." But I believe that it is vital for us to strive to develop and demonstrate these qualities because they represent what is best in all men. Doing so is necessary for us to be whole and healthy — for us to thrive and to tap into our full potential as men. It makes us better men for ourselves and better for the people around us and better for the people we care about most. It is not necessary to argue that it is best for the whole world, for that scale is too grand and complicated. It is, however, better for *our* worlds.

THE STRIKER IN DARKNESS AND LIGHT

74

The Father contends with and overcomes conceptual chaos and confusion. He must step from the world of what is known into a dim realm where options and ideas drift in disarray, where he is haunted by the mocking shadows of numberless outcomes. This is his abyss, and as Nietzsche famously suggested, he does not merely look into it — it also looks into him and becomes part of him. It is a fundamental aspect of his being.

The Striker, in his conflict with physical chaos, must overcome corporeal fear — a mortal terror of the flesh that threatens injury, pain, and death. To do the work of The Striker — to "kill the serpent" — he must be willing and able to feel and conquer his own fear, to experience and endure pain and suffering, to face the threat of death and continue to "run toward the sound of gunfire."

To become The Striker and to do the work of The Striker, he must venture beyond the boundaries of what is comfortable and safe and approach that which could hurt or even kill him. He must become the one who seeks out the serpent — the one who dares, who tucks his chin and moves toward the source of the flying fist. Fear is a natural survival instinct that protects the body from harm, but to be a warrior or even to train as a warrior, a certain amount of risk must be accepted, and the natural fear response has to be controlled and redirected. The Striker must manage fear in the way that The Father must manage confusion.

Just as The Striker is defined by his monsters, in a related and more spiritual sense he is defined by his encounters with darkness — with fear and pain and suffering and death. The Striker is initiated in darkness, and he must also be prepared to become darkness. He cannot be or become what he is without it, so this darkness is a fundamental aspect of his being.

75

Initiation into manhood has always involved facing and overcoming some form of death or pain or fear, because for much of human history, initiations into manhood have been more or less interchangeable with initiations into warring and hunting bands. Becoming an adult man meant becoming one who hunts or fights, and these initiations prepared young men for that role.

This is not limited to Indo-European cultures or mythologies. Initiation into manhood all around the world has generally involved some sort of ordeal, as well as some kind of spiritual, symbolic death. The initiate is a boy, and the boy must be die so that the man can be born. In some places, the boy is symbolically attacked by beasts, often accompanied by the sound of a bullroarer — symbolizing the voice of the sky god or even thunder — and he is forced to undergo the traumatic process of circumcision.[57] Some cultures force initiates to drink something that puts them to sleep, and then they are partially buried.

A process of initiation which is more or less universal has been broken down by anthropologists, and the three stages of initiation have been identified as "separation, margin (or *limen*, signifying "threshold in Latin), and aggregation."[58] Prospective initiates are removed from their larger communities and moved out to into a border zone, a liminal space that we can imagine physically and metaphysically as a twilight zone just beyond the light of the fire. Initiates are stripped of all former identity and status and often their clothing, and they are sometimes painted to become "ghosts" — to become the dead. Some are forced to survive on their own, or encouraged to steal. Some are stung by ants or they must stoically endure some pain or trauma. In many cases young men go into a place said to be inhabited by monsters or enter an enclosure that symbolizes the belly of some beast, where they are spiritually "consumed" and eventually emerge as men.[59]

Moving from the primitive to recent times, these patterns are repeated in gang and fraternity hazing rituals. Street gang prospects are often "beaten in" or asked to commit a crime to become full members of the group. Participants in some German and Austrian fencing fraternities still allow themselves to be struck in the face with a sword to demonstrate courage. This produces a prominent scar known as a *Schmisse*.

To reach the phase of aggregation — to become a member of the group and a full man in its estimation — young men and initiates have to demonstrate courage, and in doing so willingly, affirm the value of the group's honor and show their commitment to becoming part of the gang.

To become a man among men — which for most of human history has involved hunting and fighting, the operational domains of The Striker — men have always been expected to endure fear and pain with fortitude and abandon a weaker, more boyish and more dependent self in an ordeal that symbolized a spiritual death followed by a rebirth into full manhood as a member of the hunting and fighting gang.

This descent into darkness and encounter with death and suffering precedes but also becomes an inextricable part of their identities, and it is an inextricable part of the The Striker as an ideal form. It is this chiaroscuro, this balance between darkness and light, that renders the muscularity of The Striker and gives depth to his character.

76

When the Striker goes into darkness, he is not only dealing with death and fear, but realizing that he must be prepared to become a death-dealer and inspire fear when necessary. The idealized warrior is pictured in shining armor or dress uniform, standing at attention and ever-ready, or galloping through rays of light into battle and glory. However, the actual work of The Striker is to become terrible, to become death to his quarry and to other men, to become the alligator that seizes the deer, to become a source of chaos pointed outward to protect and champion all that which is within the perimeter of his order.

The Japanese expressed this aspect of the warrior artfully in many examples of samurai armor. The armor and particularly the face masks of men and sometimes even their horses are frequently more demonic than heroic. The author of *Hagakure* asserted that "the way of the warrior is death." The samurai embraced death, became death, and often looked like death. One imagines the terror of a man coming across these apparitions in the morning mist.

For those familiar with Germanic lore, this may bring to mind the storied transformations of the *berserkir* and *ulfheðnar* — warriors who take on the aspect of bears and wolves. Bands of such warriors were believed to fight in some kind of powerful, magical trance that made them fearless and savage — so hungry for battle and bloodshed that they "bit their shields."

Cú Chulainn, hero of Irish legend, was often described as being young and superhumanly handsome, but when seized by his berserker-like battle frenzy called "The Torque," he became animalistic and monstrous.

> "His hair stood on end: you'd think each hair had been hammered into his head. Each hair seemed tipped with a spark, so sharply did they shoot upright. He closed one eye as narrow as the eye of a needle; he opened the other as wide as the mouth of a goblet. He bared his teeth from ear to ear. He opened his gob so wide you could see the inside of his gullet. The hero's light sprang from the crown of his head." [60]

Warriors and warrior-gods are gods of the sky, but they have been repeatedly envisioned as gods of the sky in turmoil and darkness. They are gods of the wrathful heavens furiously transformed. Thor and Indra are gods of thunder and lightning and the storm, evoking the raw and dreadful fury of the powers above.

These high Strikers are the exemplars who epitomize the spirit of the fighting gang described in *The Way of Men*. This war band of men is sometimes identified as a Männerbund, a *comitatus*, or a *sodāles*.

The Maruts were Indra's war band, though they were fathered by Rudra, the wild, "roaring god," who was also associated with the wind and the storm and terror, and who is sometimes compared to aspects of Odin.[61] The Maruts personify the storm of war. Invoked as virile gods of "resistless might who love the rain, resplendent, terrible like wild beasts in their strength,"[62] it is said that "every creature is afraid" before them, and that they are "terrible to behold."[63]

Warriors may be champions of a particular order, but to do what they do, they must also become agents of chaos to other men and natural creatures. In battle, they take on the aspect of death and aim to incite terror in their enemies and all those who resist or oppose their order. They must transform themselves into fearsome creatures.

We see this throughout history, with men donning animal skins or altering their appearances to become gouls who attack in the night, as the Germanic Harii tribes did.[64] This desire to become and project death and deadliness is also evident in contemporary military culture and apparel, rife with skulls and ferocious creatures. A similarly beastly transformation is implied in the names of sports teams, as men put on images of lions, bears, cougars, gators, and even sharks — suggesting that they will ravage the other team like apex predators. Likewise, mixed martial artists often choose to cover themselves in tattoos and slogans and images associated with death and ferocity. Traditional tattoos first became popular among sailors and soldiers and biker gangs, and skulls and predators have long been staples in tattoo flash.

As young men differentiate themselves from females and identify with the warrior aspect of themselves, many gravitate toward some kind of fierce or macabre imagery. Gruesome themes and representations are found throughout all kinds of metal and rap subcultures because young men want to revel in the fantasy of becoming terrible and menacing and project an image of strength. This is both a threat display as well as an unconscious or semi-conscious acknowledgement that becoming a man has something to do with not only overcoming death, but becoming death — becoming a potential killer or source of harm.[65]

77

A warrior becomes death for outsiders, but this often makes insiders — people who live within the perimeter of his protection, the very people whom the Striker champions — uncomfortable with him or even fearful of him.

In the story of Heracles' labors in the *Library of Pseudo Apollodorus*, after Herakles slays the Nimean lion, Eurystheus is "astounded by his bravery" and refuses to allow him into the walled city. Eurystheus conveyed his requests for additional labors through a herald.

A man who has proven that he can be a threat to outsiders is also perceived as a possible threat to insiders. He has demonstrated his potential for murder. This experience alienates him from the uninitiated, who cannot fully understand what he has seen and done. Scholars of myth have observed that this awkward mix of respect and concern is a repeated mythic theme. The "second function" man is seen in a positive light in his role as a protector, but people also tend to treat warriors warily, because they recognize that the warrior's wild capacity for offensive violence is a potential threat to the community itself.[66,67]

It is easy to see this phenomenon manifest itself not only in the police, but in war and combat veterans who struggle to reintegrate into the general population after they have concluded their service. While there is a shrinking community eager to genuflect to anyone with a history of military service, there is a growing part of the civilian population keen to treat combat veterans, police and other fighters as either being damaged victims or loose canons. These tendencies tend to be self-fulfilling prophecies that either estrange such men or pollute their spirits with ressentiment, hypersentimentality, or self-pity.

Warriors become what they are on or beyond the perimeter of order. And that's where polite society wants to keep them. This hunting and fighting role on the perimeter is the root of masculinity, and civilized society has pathologized masculinity and pushed men who are good at being men out to its fringes for the same reason civilized people have always been uncomfortable with warriors inside the city walls.

"We only want you to be men when we need you — out there. In here, you're scary and you make us nervous."

78

The Striker is created in his confrontation with darkness and pain and fear, and he must be willing to become a source of chaos.

His spiritual struggle is to remain a directed source of chaos — a bolt that strikes in the service of a higher ideal or in the service of others. A bolt with purpose. Surrounded by chaos, there is always a danger that he may lose himself in it and become completely chaotic and wild and directionless and nihilistic — to go, as a friend in law enforcement recently put it, full "heart of darkness."

The role of The Striker is to become a source of chaos and to interact with it in the service of light — do go out into darkness and then return to the light. It is his purpose to become chaos to all enemies of his order — to champion his fire — but to avoid descending into a pure savage nihilism that will make him a source of chaos to everyone and everything that comes close to him. The Striker must be able to become a berserker without going completely berserk — to be thumotic without going psychotic.

The Striker is the storm, but in order for him and for the world to remain in balance, the storm must eventually be allowed to subside and give way to the light of the sun a return to its order. The "terrible" Marut, the torqued man, the wild avenger of light must return to his ordered form and take his place in the clear sky of the shining Father. As the idea of him hovers above us like an eagle, men can look up to The Striker as an exemplar of manly might and courage, endurance and excellence.

Stories about heroes inspired men and boys who have never done the work of The Striker to reach inside themselves and become a little stronger, a little more courageous, a little bit more physically excellent — and to seek, as men, the esteem of other men.

I've found in my dealings with men who are or have been Strikers that, when their storm has passed and they are done dealing with death and pain and fear, they often take an interest in working to perpetuate life. It seems to be healthy and therapeutic for them to shift their focus and find balance in the intellectual work of the Father, as leaders, or in the life-affirming work of the Lord of the Earth. When you've spent a long time focused on killing things, it makes sense to spend some time focused on growing them, and on simply enjoying being alive.

*"Prosperity we crave from thee, afar from sin and near to wealth,
tending to perfect happiness both for tomorrow and today."*

— *The Rig Veda.* Book 6 - HYMN LVI. (Pūṣaṇ)

THE LORD OF THE EARTH

Perpetuation and Prosperity

79

Men are animals.

We may look upward, and through invention and ingenuity
and the mastery of fire, we may even shoot ourselves into the
sky and the vast void of outer space. But men are beasts of the
earth, and we will always in some way be bound to it. We are
not airy spirits but creatures of flesh and blood who have to eat
and sleep and drink to survive. Men can make babies in test
tubes, but reproduction is an ultimate cause, and the ability to
circumvent our more mammalian means of insemination in
no way relieves us of our pressing and visceral desire to fuck.
Our animal bodies stimulate us to actions that perpetuate our
survival with appetites, and these appetites are an inextricable
part of our psyches. Freud would have associated many of these
appetites with the "Id."

In themselves, these appetites are not evil or contrary to our
nature, but part of it. When uncontrolled, appetites may become
compulsions that lead to gluttony, greed, addiction, unnecessary
drama, and disease, but satisfying and even occasionally
indulging these appetites is also what makes life joyful.

Prosperity is not mere survival or subsistence, but the enjoyment of plenty. We could live on tasteless nutrient paste, but fine foods make life more pleasurable. We could get by wearing rags, but it is better to have higher quality and more aesthetically pleasing clothing. We could live in huts and tents, but human prosperity is so often associated with magnificent works of architecture and craftsmanship. Human relationships are also necessary for us to function within groups. Men are social animals, and we not only want but are happiest and most fulfilled when we build and maintain higher-quality relationships.

The Father is concerned with order. The Striker is the weapon of that order — he fights physical chaos to impose that order and create an ordered zone of safety within which human life can prosper.

The Lord of the Earth manages and shapes the material and social chaos of everyday life to perpetuate life and order and promote prosperity. He is an intermediary between earth and sky who brings natural and human resources into the harmonious service of The Father's cosmic order and human flourishing. The Lord of the Earth is a patron of the tribe and the people, representing the spirit of the working man — from shepherds and stock-breeders to farmers, artisans, and merchants. He represents all of the work that must be done to satisfy our basic animal needs and wants and, in exceeding them, bring joy into the world around us.

80

There is evidence of what has been called a "pastoral" god in various traditions, and his proposed name in Proto-Indo-European is *péh₂usōn. Linguistically, he has been linked to the familiar pastoral Greek god Pan and in Sanskrit, Pūṣan, who is associated with marriages, journeys, roads, cattle and wealth. Both gods are linked to goats, as Pūṣan drives a chariot pulled by goats, and Pan is traditionally depicted with the horns and the lower body of a goat.[68] The root *péh₂-* has been alternately interpreted as meaning "to nourish,"[69] "to guard or cause to graze (shepherd)."[70] The name of the Sanskrit god Pūṣan is sometimes translated as "nourisher," and his functions overlap with Pan's functions as a god of shepherds, and some of the functions of Pan's father, Hermes. Hermes is also depicted with sheep and lambs in addition to variously being a trickster and a messenger of the gods, as well as a god associated with commerce, social exchange, and crossing boundaries.[71]

These pastoral gods are related to the occupations of herding and breeding livestock that were especially important in early Indo-European societies. In Iranian, the occupations of "pasturing" and "stock-breeding" were unified in a word that identified the social class of men who did that work: *vāstryō fšuyant*. This name corresponds to the Indic term *vaiśya*, which became one of the four castes or varnas in Hinduism, identifying agriculturalists and merchants, and essentially meaning a man who is a member of the tribe.[72] This social class was later represented in Ancient Greece by the Hóplēs, artisans associated with the smith god Hephaistos, and Argádēs, who were farmers associated with Poseidon, who was a patron of agriculture as well as the god of the sea.[73] Njörðr, the Germanic god of the sea, was also associated with crop fertility and was the father of the fertility god Freyr, so there is some conceptual overlap and continuity there as well.

In early Roman lore, some of The Lord of the Earth's functions were handled by the community god Quirinus, "patron of men as producers and progenitors,"[74] who seems to have had a kindred spirit in the Celtic Teutātes, the god of the people.[75] Indeed, while comparatively little is known about the Celtic system, a tripartite system may have existed among the Celts that is much like the system being presented in this book — with Esus being good and "all-competent," Taranis serving as the thundering solar warrior god, and Teutātes as god of the tribe or everyday man.[76] A horned god of nature and animals, more similar to Pan, also seems to have been celebrated by the Celts using the name Cernunnos.

There is a parallel to this "god of the people" in the Vedic Aryaman, who is also connected to the Airyaman — indicating a member of the community or tribe — in the Zoroastrian tradition. In *The Rig Veda*, Aryaman is most often invoked in addition to the first function gods Mitra and Varuna in contexts related to law and worldly concerns.

We could call this god *$*péh_2usōn$*, but I believe it is more important for these ideals to be immediately accessible. They should feel current and alive, not unnecessarily arcane — though that does have its own charm. As I mentioned earlier, the Germanic god Freyr's name comes from the Proto-Germanic *frawjô*, which meant "lord." In modern English, Lord is often used as a synonym for "god," which is in this case somewhat appropriate. However, in a feudal context, a lord was not necessarily a king, but the head and manager of a large estate, under a king's rule. These estates included farmers and craftsmen and produced food and goods that sustained the broader community. Kings don't manage farmers and craftsmen; they set policy, deal with "big picture" issues, and manage lords — who manage farmers and craftsmen. For our purposes, this lord reigns over the realm of the earth and earthly concerns. Like The Striker, he serves the sacred order of the father-sovereign.

While in various pantheons, craftsmen, and farmers and traders and herdsmen may have had more specific gods, the integrated ideal of the Lord of the Earth oversees all of these activities. Like a feudal lord, he is closer to the land and to those who produce and trade than the lofty king. In a podcast conversation I had with Old Norse scholar Matthias Nordvig, he suggested that the Vanir and Freyr may have been relatively late additions to the Germanic pantheon.[77] Even if that is true, I believe that Freyr was a necessary addition to complete the tripartite system and represent the totality of men's inner and outer concerns. As animals, no matter how high or tactically minded we are, we still spend most of our lives engaged in processes that sustain and perpetuate life.

Freyr is also paired with his twin sister, Freya, and this illustrates a larger theme in myth that associates the earth and fertility with women and female deities. "Mother Earth" itself is generally represented as a feminine entity, as with the Greek Gaia and to some extent, her daughter Rhea, the mother of Zeus and the original Olympians. The goddess Demeter is also associated with fertility and the harvest, as are countless other goddesses in other pantheons. The earth is also linked to both the womb and death — as it is from the earth and darkness that we emerge, and to which we all return. The earth is also the void and chaos, the raw material from which men make order. If we see the earth as a fertile woman, man must learn her ways and interact with her to sustain and perpetuate life and prosperity.

Freya represents the female aspect of this interaction, and Freyr represents the male experience and perspective. In some sense, men and women are "twins" who issue from the same source, opposite but complementary, each requiring the other to achieve a unified purpose — like a plug and a socket. We are concerned here with men and their ideals and masculine psychology, so I will leave the female side of that equation for someone else to address.

81

It is said that "Frey is the most splendid of the gods. He controls the rain and the shining of the sun, and through them the bounty of the earth. It is good to invoke him for peace and abundance. He also determines men's success in prosperity."[78] Adam of Bremen wrote that he "bestows peace and pleasure on mortals" and noted that he is often shown with a gigantic phallus, a detail which recalls other male fertility gods, such as the Greek Priapus.

Peace, pleasure, the bounty of the earth, prosperity...that's a wide range of responsibilities and a lot of hats to wear, but the work of the Lord of the Earth is concerned with both the practical details of life and the enjoyment of life itself. When principles and ideals and laws are in place, in the spaces between wars and expansions and responses to threats, there is a lot of work that must be done simply to keep life going.

What kinds of things do you have to do every day to keep things going? And on a broader scale, what kinds of occupations and customs and events are or have been necessary to keep things going? What kinds of things need to be done to keep people invested? And what kinds of things make life better — what kinds of things improve your quality of life?

These things that make life better are both material and emotional — and material objects often affect our emotional sense of well being. There is much to be said for discipline and loyalty and identity, but if you can't offer the people around you a better holistic quality of life than they can find elsewhere, they may seek out another group or leader who can. If you want people to be productive and keep them invested in your project, whatever it is, you have to improve their lives in a variety of ways.

Improving people's lives requires all kinds of work that isn't as lofty, abstract, and high status as the work of the sovereign-creator or as glorious and heroic as the warrior's work. But it is essential, all the same. And this work applies not only to business and tribe but also to family and friends. What kind of experience are you providing for the people around you, and how are you improving their overall quality of life? What kind of exchange are you providing — how much reciprocity is there?

To visualize the Lord of the Earth as an ideal and define his domain, think about Abraham Maslow's "Hierarchy of Needs," first conceived in a paper published in 1943.

Maslow believed that our needs as human animals begin with basic physiological needs such as food and shelter and sex and safety. When those basic needs are satisfied, our needs become more emotional and abstract. When we are safe, and our hungers have been satiated, we care more about social relationships and intimacy, and community. When those needs are met, we concern ourselves with esteem and accomplishment, and beyond that, we seek "self-actualization." Self-actualization involves the realization of our potentials and the expression of our gifts and talents. As he wrote, "A musician must make music, an artist must paint, a poet must write if he is to be ultimately happy. What a man can be, he must be."[79] Later in life, Maslow apparently aimed self-actualization more toward the transcendent.

There is no need to think of this hierarchy as a strict progression. While it is true that if we're starving and our safety is threatened, the more emotional and abstract needs don't matter much, but if the most basic needs are met, the others seem to fluctuate in importance as circumstances change. For instance, one could be highly esteemed and fairly self-actualized, but the loss of a relationship or family member could increase the immediate importance of meeting that need. What is relevant for our purposes here is to look at all of the needs that the people around us have as a whole.

Many men tend to focus on the most basic requirements of life and discount the importance of the others. Men who are particularly oriented toward being warriors tend to concentrate on tactical and survival-oriented concerns.

82

The Lord of the Earth and Freyr and Pan all of the other pastoral gods and fertility gods of the people tend to be associated with natural growth. They are connected with the crops, flocks, herds, boars and antlered herbivores that have provided sustenance and become symbols of prosperity for men throughout history. The Lord of the Earth personifies the way that man accesses the resources of the natural world and tends to them and even shapes them over time to ensure their growth.

Some men are extremely connected to the land and the natural world. But just we're not all going to be warriors... we're not all going to be farmers, either.

Gardening and farming and managing herds are real occupations, but they can be made relevant for all of us by viewing them metaphorically. We can access and express and act on this spirit of perpetuation simply by looking at what we have, tending to it, and encouraging its growth. Whether we're talking about automobiles or homes or investments, our assets need to be maintained and developed continually. Books need to be balanced, and bills need to be paid, and oil needs changing. There are so many things we have to do simply to keep the things that we have going. These tasks are all necessary to ensure continued prosperity. We all have our own fields of wheat and our own sheep to tend.

If we step back and look at the big picture, there isn't much difference between a man who turns a shovel and a man who turns a wrench, between a man who drives cattle and a man who runs wires, or even the man who does all of their accounting. All of those men learned a trade or a craft that they employ to sustain life and prosperity — to keep things going. Achilles' armor was made by Hephaestus, the god of blacksmiths and makers. The craftsmen, the builders, and the merchants, as well as the farmers and herders fall within Dumézil's third function and so do all of the myriad gods and ideals that keep the material world moving to perpetuate life and order.

While our material responsibilities may be obvious and pressing, all of our relationships require the same type of ongoing maintenance. Romantic relationships, business relationships, friendships, relationships with family members and children, and even relationships with pets have to be regularly maintained if they are going to continue to be productive. If you love someone or respect someone professionally or value their friendship, you have to continue to invest time in that relationship in the same way that you have to feed livestock or water plants if you want to keep them alive and make them grow. You have to tell people that you love them or care about them or value them as associates, not because you need to hear it back, but because people want to hear that and know that and feel valued. Everyone has emotional needs. If you want to promote growth and perpetuate your relationships to make your own life happier and more successful, you have to continually put in the time and do the work of attending to all of the needs in the hierarchy — not just the bare minimum needed to keep people alive. Do your friends and associates feel valued and included and accomplished and self-actualized? You can help them meet and exceed their own emotional needs and achieve their own goals, without pushing them to do things they don't truly want to do or allowing them to take advantage of you or disrespect you. Unless they suffer from jealousy or have emotional problems that have nothing to do with you, your relationships with the people in your life are going to become more fruitful.

Tending to the relationships in your life means spending time doing things with or for other people. That may mean attending a function you don't want to go to or watching a film you don't want to see or helping a friend move. While engaging in these activities for the benefit of others may take time away from things that you'd rather be doing, these are necessary short-term sacrifices in the service of a long-term outcome. In that way, it's not much different from going to the gym when you don't feel like it. Doing something you don't necessarily want to do with someone whom you value — for their benefit — is a sacrifice of time and energy made so that you can continue to reap the benefits of rich, healthy, positive relationships in your life.

As I conceptualized Freyr and eventually the more culturally universal ideal that he represents as a "lord" who cultivates these kinds of relationships and networks, I started to humorously classify these little sacrifices of time and effort for others in my own mind as "doing the Lord's work."

83

Sexual reproduction is both the physical means through which we perpetuate our species and our primary metaphor for fertility and perpetuation. Fertility gods like Freyr and Priapus are sculpted with big, hard cocks, and they have been invoked by men and women to promote love and sexual gratification and reproduction.

That moment of insemination and creation is, conceptually speaking, the work of The Father—the masculine sky that mates with the feminine earth to start new worlds and new orders and create new men and women.

The Lord of the Earth and fertility gods are better understood as facilitators in this process, who spark attractions, loosen inhibitions, and make love and sex and sensuality pleasurable and appealing. Perhaps for this reason, the rustic fertility gods are not only gods of nature, but very often gods of wine, like Dionysus with his entourage of maenads and lusty satyrs. The Lord of the Earth is not the procreator, but the smile and the wink and the twinkle in the eye. He eases the moment of abandon when we allow our earthy animal natures to rise up from the depths of Id and overcome our egos and superegos and let that dark, wild horse pull the chariot wherever it wants for a while.

In one of the hymns to Dionysus, the twice-born god is captured by sailors, who try to bind him, but his fetters fall to the ground. Wine bubbles up from the bottom of the boat and vines grow up the mast, blooming into berries and flowers. Then Dionysus becomes a lion and roars, and all of the sailors jump into the sea and become dolphins. The wise old helmsman remains, and Dionysus saves him. The hymn ends with the singer singing that anyone who forgets Dionysus "forgets how to compose a sweet song."[80] It's a fantastic image illustrating the nature of the god, who comes unbound, unleashes a beautiful chaos, and allows the animal inside to roar.

Allowing our animal natures to out and roar every so often is one of the pleasures of being alive.

84

It is the Lord's nature and duty to be more sensitive to the natural world and its cycles, to the concerns of women and children, to the emotional and material needs and wants of his peers and charges. The Father must be benevolent but strict. The Striker must remain somewhat distant and detached, hardened and practical, stoic, and disciplined. It is the work of the Lord to get closer to the ground and to the people around him, to mix with the people inside the perimeter and feel what they feel. The Lord is more empathic, and in our system he would be closest to Moore's "Lover."

Moore's characterization of the Lover and, by extension, the artist and poet and the musician — whom he offers as exemplars of the archetype — seems to have been influenced by the rebellious individualism of 19th Century Romanticism, and the trope of the artist as an effeminate "bleeding heart" socialist subversive that has persisted in prominence well into the 21st Century. Moore describes the man under the influence of the Lover — typically the artist type — as being at odds with all socially created boundaries and in a state of conflict between emotional passion and order.

I see this conflict as the creative aspect of the king/magician seeking outlet and chafing against pre-existing structure. In the way that that there is something in some warriors that must overthrow a king to become kings themselves, there is something in the artist that wants to tear down boundaries so that he can draw his own. As Moore noted, the energy of this archetype can at first glance seem "utterly opposed" to the energies of the warrior and the "King's concerns for boundaries, containment, order, and discipline." The artist/lover is concerned with feelings and empathy. This makes sense and fits within our paradigm. However, it is important to determine whose feelings are most important to a given artist or lover, who he is empathizing with, and where his loyalties lie.

In the case of this "sensitive" type, there is often an unresolved conflict with or anger toward a father or father figure or male peer group that manifests as misandry. The sensitive type feels excluded or undervalued by men — men who are good at being men — and directs his empathy and sentimentality toward women or others he perceives to be similarly excluded or undervalued. As a man, the thumotic aspect of his nature finds what he believes to be a noble fight in correcting this perceived injustice, exclusion, or undervaluation. This is one of the reasons why men who have unresolved conflicts with more masculine peers or father figures frequently become champions of ideologies based in victimhood and ressentiment.

Over the past century or so, this tendency was affirmed and given outlet in social circles and power structures associated with various mutations of Marxism -- to the point that it has become "expected" that the sensitive, artistic type is also an opponent of existing social orders, hierarchical standards of beauty, and the masculine virtues themselves.

For the majority of history, the most prominent works of art celebrated the differences between the sexes and the dominant myths, values, and ideals — the flames — of the culture. Men, as subjects of art, were masculine and heroic. The artists and craftsmen of old strove to capture and idealize strength and beauty and the beauty of strength, values which are always by their very nature exclusive and hierarchical.

When it became *de rigueur* for art and artists to be subversive, the artworks produced became increasingly ugly and disordered and antithetical to the natural strength-based values of men. As this trend continued and compounded, a jealous sickness of the soul infected the creative community and the sick were increasingly drawn to it. So much of what is called "art" today is anti-order, anti-strength, and so fundamentally anti-male that it has become commonplace for men to say that they don't like art, or that they don't like "modern" art. The reason why they say that they don't like "art" is because the "art" world doesn't like them!

Art and artisans don't need to have an oppositional relationship with men and masculinity, or with father-figures and warriors — in fact, it is historically unusual. When men who are more sensitive or artistic resolve their anger toward fathers and men who are good (or better) at being men, they can make a powerful contribution to the perpetuation of order, beauty, and virility. When we look back to the great men past for inspiration, it is the images that artists and artisans have created that give these exemplars forms in our imaginations. We visualize them through paintings and statues or by remembering descriptive lines penned by long-dead poets. Who would know the name of Achilles or care about the voyage of Odysseus, were it not for a Homer? The sounds of war and courage, adventure, and glory were made memorable motifs by men like Holst and Wagner. They are reimagined and reinvigorated today by the likes of Hans Zimmer, who has spent a career writing and recording the soundtracks for the supermen who fight chaos and disorder in our cinematic dreamscapes.

To create art that is truly moving and powerful, the artist must be sensitive to not only his own emotions, but to the emotions of others and he must make contact with something eternal, and be able to direct all of that emotional energy in a way that connects with his intended audience. When the artist listens to the voices and the spirits of the narcissistic, of the chaotic, of the resentful and disaffected, of the weak and the cowardly and the sick and the hateful, or when he only listens to women — he produces art which is naturally repellent to men. When the artist is able to empathize with men and makes himself an ally of masculine virtue, he produces work that is strong and beautiful and capable of elevating other men and inspiring them to greatness. He uses his talents and the raw materials found in the world around him to produce art that in itself perpetuates solar order and virility.

This, too, is the Lord's work.

85

However, elevation and inspiration are not the sole purposes of art. Poetry and theater and song are also produced for pleasure and release. So are many crafts, such as the production of wine and spirits and the cooking of fine foods. There is a life-despising mentality that hates all luxury and indulgence and carnal pleasure — but the Lord of this Earth will have none of that. There is no doubt a time for discipline and one must keep an eye on pleasures that can too easily become vices, but when the Lord of the Earth takes his rightful place under the sun, he is the patron of ordered and organized release and enjoyment. The people of the ancient worlds held many feasts and festivals, but they were all finite.

Today we have access to far more highly stimulating foods and goods and entertainment than our ancestors did. Even the poor have access to foods that would have been special desserts, with exorbitantly high sugar content, or high-calorie savory foods with a relatively low nutrient value, which are designed to taste extremely good. In fact, in many cases, the poorest people live in areas regarded as "food deserts," where they have better access to fast food and convenience store "treats" than they have to healthier and more nutritious foods. The same is true of so many things that, like tasty food, make our monkey brains happy. Most people have access to massive amounts of pornography, cheap television entertainment (a 24-hour nonstop "theater" production), addictive video games, and access to a stream of music that keeps playing forever. People who have more money can have almost anything they can imagine delivered to them, often at the touch of a button, and can enjoy comforts at home that would have amazed royalty only a few decades ago. So many of these luxuries are carefully engineered to dose us with dopamine and marketed to keep us coming back for more.

One of the challenges of modernity is that it is all too easy to live in a state of perpetual feast and festival. Everything that stimulates is encouraged and accessible. We must actively seek out and prioritize that which is substantive and strengthening to avoid being swept up in a deluge of wine and sensuality. Life without Dionysus would be dreary, but the endless and disordered service of appetites is chaotic, destructive, and exhausting.

Sensible men seem to agree that while Las Vegas can be a good time, more than two or three days and nights on The Strip is too much.

86

The chariots of men's souls are pulled by two horses. The horse of noble — of higher — origin is animated by thumos. The horse of lower origin, who comes from a place closer to the earth and the chaotic oblivion of pre (or post) existence, is animated by appetite. Both horses can run wild and become unruly unless they are reigned in by the logos of the charioteer and placed in the service of solar order.

To realize his potential as a Striker, a hero like Herakles must pass over the cheap allure of vice and choose a path of discipline that gestures toward perfection — the harder way of Areté, of excellence. The Striker's excellences require a development of the tactical virtues and the mastery of the skills required to do battle. He trains and disciplines himself or allows himself to be trained and disciplined to increase his strength and courage and to acquire a skills particular skill set, and, guided by logos, his righteous, spirited assertiveness and anger are directed service of a higher order and purpose, to contend with physical chaos.

To realize his potential as a Lord of the Earth, a man must also choose between excellence and vice. When the thumotic Striker runs amok, the potential negative outcome is impulsive, unjust, and pointless violence and murder. The Lord of the Earth is animated by appetite, so he can descend into overindulgence, addiction, and dissolution when unrestrained. He is prone to hypersensuality, intense passion, greed, and gluttony.

There is a story about Lord Freyr from the *Prose Edda* that I sometimes refer to as "Freyr's Error." Freyr sat on Odin's high seat Hliðskjálf, from which as you will recall, one can see all things. Looking down on Jötunheimr, he saw a female jötunn named Gerðr. He was overcome by her beauty, and became obsessed with this female, who was a stranger to him. Believing that she was unattainable, he became depressed. Eventually, Freyr tried to convince his manservant Skírnir go to Jötunheimr to seduce Gerðr on his behalf. Skírnir asked for Freyr's magical sword, which fought by itself, as payment for this deed, and Freyr hastily agreed and gave Skírnir the sword. After threatening her with curses, Skírnir eventually did convince Gerðr to hook up with (and presumably marry) Freyr. Eventually, Freyr was forced to fight without a sword, using an antler instead, and it was foretold that he would meet his end for the lack of it at Ragnarok.

Freyr gave up an extremely useful and practical asset and tool — his magical sword — because he was overcome with lust for a woman he barely knew. I'm sure the story sounds familiar, even if you've never read the Eddas. We all know a man who has far too quickly given up far more than he should have because he became infatuated with a woman...and that story almost never ends well. The same potential for foolish and impulsive waste exists in all of man's impulses and appetites.

87

Just as a warrior animated by thumos develops excellences that are ideally employed to champion order, when a man works in accordance with good order to meet and exceed human needs and appetites, he develops excellences in craft and productivity aimed at making people's lives joyful while also elevating their minds and spirits.

The word *virtus* in Latin and the word *areté* in Greek both began as terms which indicated martial valor and various excellences in the manly arts of war. However, in times of peace and as these cultures thrived, those words both acquired broader meanings. The root of the word areté is the same root that produced the word *áristos*, from which we get the word aristocracy, which means "rule by the best or most fitting."[81] Historian Werner Jaeger wrote that, "it was natural for the Greeks, who ranked every man according to his ability, to use the same standard for the world in general. That is why they could apply the word areté to things and beings which were not human, and that is why the content of the word grew richer in later times."[82] Excellence can be found in many people and practices and things. Likewise, while its root comes from a word for man (*wiHrós) and originally meant martial manliness, the idea of virtue eventually expanded to include a wide range of moral and social virtues. The practice and perfecting of skills and conduct are not limited to the fighting aspect of man. The work of perpetuation also requires the practice and perfecting of skills and conduct. Recalling Herakles' choice between the way of Areté and Kakia, Xenophon noted that "if you want your land to produce abundant crops, you must look after your land; if you expect to make money from your livestock, you must take care of your livestock."[83]

When toiling in the service of righteous order, the aspect of man that perpetuates — idealized here in the Lord of the Earth — must also practice and perfect his crafts and himself. This is his excellence, his discipline, his virtue, and areté. The Lord of the Earth represents the farmer who learns more about farming with every season so that he can produce more and higher quality crops that bring sustenance and joy to his peers and his people. He is the artful potter and the skilled stonemason. The Lord of the Earth is the virtuoso musician who practices his art tirelessly so that he can perform better and watch out of the corner of his eye as the men and women around him lose themselves and get caught up in his audible magic. He is present in the careful carpenter and the diligent bookkeeper and even the industrious businessman. The Lord of the Earth presses fine wine and prepares fantastic feasts. He is the butcher and the baker, the manager and the mechanic, the programmer and the poet. The Lord of the Earth does the work to keep things going, to perpetuate life and to make life worth living — and he attends to this fine and worthy work with an undying passion for excellence.

ᛉ *Maðr er manns gaman*
ok moldar auki
ok skipa skreytir.
homo mildingr.

—Icelandic Rune Poem

THE LORD'S SYMBOLS

88

Upward Reaching Plant Life

The Lord of the Earth represents the part of man that rises from the earth and is rooted in it, but which looks upward to the light and toward order. So perhaps the most obvious symbols of his nature are trees, sustaining wheat and productive grasses, and fruitful and flowering plants that similarly reach upward toward the sun and simultaneously bring beauty and pleasure to life on the ground.

The Symbol of Perpetuation and "The Higher Choice"

The symbol I have used in this book to represent The Lord of the Earth began with the double Algiz bindrune rune that I have been associating with the god Freyr for years. Algiz (ᛉ) is a Germanic rune that in the Elder Futhark probably means "elk." In the Younger Futhark, the same symbol (ᛉ), named Maðr, evokes "man."

In the Icelandic Rune poem, man is described as "the delight

of man, the augmentation of the earth, and adorner of ships,"
which tidily describes some of the roles of The Lord of the
Earth. Man is a social creature, and as the saying also repeated
in the Old Norse Hávamál goes, *maður er manns gaman* — "man
is the delight of man." Within our own tribes and circles, things
are best when we enrich each other's lives. Men augment the
earth for each other by taking its resources and shaping them
to increase their abundance, as with the cultivation of crops
and the domestication and husbandry of animals. And we are
adorners of ships, who take that which is simply necessary and
make it beautiful. The Algiz rune also resembles a tree or a man
standing with his arms outstretched in a receptive or worshipful
upward-facing orientation.

This double Algiz bindrune was initially formulated for a ritual
speech designed to inspire men to take "the higher choice." What
I meant by this at the time and what I mean still is that in the
midst of abundance, we have access to a wide variety of choices.
We are often encouraged to take the easy option or the cheap
high, the junk food, the trashy entertainment. There are usually
higher, more elevating and enriching and nutritive choices
available, but they are often more expensive in some way or
less immediately gratifying. Stacked on top of one another, the
double Algiz creates a Fehu or Fé (ᚠ) rune, faced by its reflection.
In the rune poems, ᚠ evokes wealth, and the name of the rune
in an earlier form, going all the way back to the Proto-Indo-
European (*péku*), means cattle or livestock - on of the earliest
forms of meaningful wealth. "F" is also the letter that begins the
god Freyr's name, which again means "lord."

A Lord has or creates wealth — and you can be as philosophical
as you want about what wealth means to you. For the purposes
of the symbolism here, any kind of desirable abundance or even
a natural gift or a lot of good luck will do. When you have wealth
of any kind, you can use it or spend it on cheap and trivial thrills,
or you can take the higher choice and do something productive

with it — something "productive" usually means something that directly or indirectly benefits not only your own happiness and development but the happiness and development of the people around you. The reflected ᚠ could be viewed as a representation of the lure of the impoverished soul who uses squanders abundance by making "lower" choices.

The double Algiz, double Fehu bindrune also reminds one somewhat of wheat or a tree or some form of "upward reaching plant life" — something rooted in the earth and oriented toward the sky.

The symbols used for The Father, The Striker, and The Lord of the Earth in this book all fit within the same solar circle and follow similar lines. All of the symbols emanate outward from the same center and symbolically fit into a circular containment representing the perimeter of sacred order. In its totality, The Lord of the Earth's symbol represents outward growth and perpetuation from a holy center, as well as the concepts associated with the higher choice bindrune, the pursuit of excellence in craft, and the well-ordered enjoyment of earthly appetites.

Mead, Wine, Beer, Spirits, and Other Symbols of Intoxication

In early myths surrounding Zeus's cults on the island of Crete, it was believed that he was born to the goddess Rhea in a cave. That cave emitted a fiery glow, and swarming bees inhabited it — said to be "the nurses of Zeus." The honey in the cave may have symbolized the divine blood remaining from his birth.[84] Honey was long thought to be sacred to the gods, and it seems likely that the fermentation of honey to produce the alcoholic drink known as mead preceded the widespread cultivation of wine grapes and the production of wine. As Dionysus was more directly associated with both harvest and joyful intoxication, and his staff — the thyrsus — dripped with honey. So, in the earliest cults, this son of Zeus may have been a god of mead before he became a god of wine. Of course, he is better known from extant literature as a god of wine and the vine, as was his Roman counterpart, Bacchus.

Mead, wine, beer, and spirits are all special fruits of the harvest, and their alcoholic content imparts to them a touch of magic and a method of altering perception in a pleasurable way. It is easy to see how they might be perceived as gifts from the gods as a reward for hard work, to be imbibed in the celebration of life and renewal. A gesture reminiscent of this can even be seen in the Catholic sacrament of communion, in which wine is magically made into the blood of god in the context of ritual in a process called transubstantiation.

Honey, honeycombs, grapes, vines, and the wheat used to make beer or spirits — anything associated with the produce or the processes used to create fermented beverages could be reasonably associated with the Lord of the Earth.

There have been theories floated for some time and by many people that our earliest ancestors may have used psychedelic mushrooms in ritual. Some have even suggested that Soma, the Vedic drink of the gods, may have had something to do with "magic mushrooms." Whether that is true or not, it seems reasonable to associate something that rises from the earth and which can produce an altered, ecstatic state with the Lord of the Earth. Marijuana is also certainly not new. While it is not traditionally associated with any of the gods I've named, when used intentionally or ritually or in the context of celebration rather than habitual addiction, it fits the same pattern. We live in a new world and have access to many things. The concepts are eternal, but the particulars and how they are expressed always evolve according to the times.

The Thyrsus

As mentioned above, the thyrsus was a staff carried by Dionysus and his (usually female) cultists. It has been depicted in sculptures and pottery. It has traditionally been described as a staff, sometimes of giant fennel, topped with a pinecone, often wound with ribbon and ivy and dripping with honey. The pinecone is obviously a symbol of reproduction and the fruitfulness of the natural world.

Phallic Imagery

It has been said that Freyr was often depicted as having a giant phallus, and this is evident in sculptures like the Rällinge statuette found in Sweden. The same is true of other pastoral fertility gods, like the greek Priapus and his siblings, the Satyrs, who were generally portrayed with prominent erections. This is simple and direct symbolism associated with male fertility and the pleasure and excitement of sexual intercourse.

To depict the Lord of the Earth as having a great big boner would be conceptually and historically consistent and valid. Unfortunately, we currently live in a hypersexualized age of abundant pornography, and in America that age emerged from a highly puritanical culture. The conflict between these two extremes makes it challenging to depict many elements of human sexuality without being perceived as a purveyor of base pornography. Further, the widespread and open acceptance of homosexuality creates an environment in which a phallic symbol's intent can be easily confused. So, while phallic imagery is historically normal and conceptually coherent in the invocation of pastoral and fertility gods, at present, phallic representations should be used carefully and sparingly and with clearly defined context.

Elk, Deer, Goats, and Boars

The Celtic god Cernunnos was depicted as having antlers growing from his head, and his name may come from a word for horn. He was also shown surrounded by animals and ostensibly in harmony with them, in a way that reminds me of St. Francis of Assisi — highlighting his closeness with and connection to the natural world. This idea of a horned god has been assimilated into modern Wicca to represent masculine virility, and the idea of some archetypal horned god seems to hold a special place in the erotic imaginations of women. Freyr was forced to fight with an antler, which makes him similar to a sparring stag or a bull elk. As this antler wrestling is part of the animals' mating ritual, antlers are also associated with fertility. Deer and Elk have long been the quarry of hunters, and as trophies, their antlers are both symbols of man's mastery of nature and his intimate relationship with it.

It has been mentioned that Pūṣaṇ drove a chariot pulled by goats, and Pan was most often depicted with the horns of a goat, as were the later Roman fauns and the Roman god Faunus — a god of the forests and the fields. Like elk and deer, goats and sheep probably became fertility symbols because of their conspicuous rutting behaviors. While deer and elk seem noble and serene, and sheep appear to be more passive, there is something about the behavior of goats that is more obviously mischievous and playful. It is easy to imagine how they became more closely associated with human sexual abandon. As Christians distinguished themselves from pagans, the horned gods were probably demonized and associated with the devil to emphasize the Christian virtue of chastity.

Boars are directly associated with the fertility god Freyr in the Germanic tradition, who rode the golden boar Gullinbursti. However, boars are also portrayed as wild and terrible monsters, and therefore linked to war, so they could theoretically be associated with both the Striker and the Lord of the Earth.

"All see, and most admire, the glare which hovers round the external trappings of elevated office. To me there is nothing in it, beyond the lustre which may be reflected from its connection with a power of promoting human felicity."

— George Washington

WASHINGTON

89

As beasts of the earth, men look upward for ideals, direction, and stars to guide them. In the darkness — in the absence of stars — men will seek them out in stories or invent them by reasoning out perfect forms and paragons to the best of their ability. This book is about eternal ideals that outshine any given man — the father beyond fathers, the warrior beyond warriors, the lord of all lords. From our high seats, we have searched time and space, looking back thousands of years and faraway, through ancient myths and philosophies, hunting overlaps and consistencies, and there is still so much more to see, even after common truths have risen in sharp relief. It is impossible to know if any particular group of men in the past received these truths and fashioned them into gods, or if they elevated the memories of the best men they knew and polished away their imperfections. So many of our ideals and exemplars are known only from the recopied remainders of parchments, weathered bronzes, or chunks of crumbling stone.

However, while writing this book, it occurred to me that there is one man who lived only a little more than two hundred years ago who embodied not only the attributes of The Father but also those of The Striker and The Lord of the Earth. George Washington was only a man, and we have access to most of his letters and know enough about him to see that he was fallible and human. His story is even more relevant and inspiring because he struggled with the kinds of problems and dilemmas with which all men struggle — on the grandest imaginable scale. As I studied his biography, I was consistently humbled by his achievements and found it difficult to imagine how any man could have handled the challenges of such a life better or in a more dignified and admirable way. In fact, while one could spend a lifetime reading about the world's sky fathers in myth, doctrine, and theory — I can recommend no better real and practical earthly exemplar of The Father than I found in Ron Chernow's biography of Washington.

George Washington was born into modest wealth, and he trained first as a surveyor — a drawer of lines and separations. He became a Freemason at twenty, and the "Grand Architect of the Universe" revered by that fraternal order has much in common conceptually with the ideal of The Father. His older brother Lawrence was a colonial officer in the British military, and he aspired to a military career fighting for the crown. Washington distinguished himself as a soldier and leader in the French and Indian War. However, he was dismissively passed over for promotions because American-born subjects were held in low regard by officers born in England. After the war, he returned to civilian life, married well, and expanded his estate. He entered into local politics and served in the Virginia Provincial legislature and a wide variety of other civic and religious organizations. As a well-respected colonial war hero, landowner, and politician, Washington became a pivotal figure in the opposition to the British Parliament's treatment of its colonial subjects. After the Revolutionary War began, his peers selected him to serve as commander in chief of the Continental Army. While he was not the most experienced or necessarily the most successful commander in terms of strategy, his most outstanding achievement during the war was managing to keep a largely inexperienced and unprofessional army made up of men from different colonies fighting together against what was the wealthiest and most capable military power in the world at that time-- despite massive shortages of cash, food, clothing, and ammunition. After the Americans won the war, while he was wildly popular in the new nation and many believed that he could and should become its ruler -- possibly even its king -- he famously resigned his commission as commander and returned home to Virginia to manage his farms and business interests. As a unifying figure, he was asked to oversee the development of the republic's Constitution. After it was ratified, he was elected as the first President of the United States of America.

George Washington's story follows many of the mythic patterns associated with The Father, and he demonstrated the noble qualities of character that one would be demanded, expected, and admired in a man tasked with leading.

Washington was an ascended Striker — a fighting member of a warrior class who led a "continental kshatriya" to victory. He was physically imposing, athletic, and known for showing extraordinary courage in battle. Like Zeus and other Strikers fated to become Fathers, he led a war of rebellion against an old and tyrannical order, overcame it, and oversaw the creation and administration of a new order. Washington and the men around him started a new world, igniting and drawing out the lines of a new American mandala.

Unlike many rulers, Washington did not inherit his rank as commander or the title of President. He was elevated to the role by virtue of his character and merit, by an assembly of his peers representing various contingents of an intertribal confederacy. This is similar to the way it is sometimes theorized that the early Germanic tribes picked chieftains and the way it's been suggested that the earliest people in the Rig Vedic period elected a *rajan*.[85] The specific details regarding how ancient peoples selected their leaders are unknowable, but the correlation between Washington and ancient predecessors would represent an interesting return to pre-monarchic form. Washington could also be compared to what anthropologists call a tribal "big man" — a leader who gains influence through establishing trust, making wise decisions, and mediating disputes to reach the best outcome for the greatest good.

George Washington adopted and cared for several children, but he had no biological children of his own. Instead, he became referred to as the "father of his country" and one of its "founding fathers." He participated in and ultimately oversaw the process of structuring the government and the culture of a new order from post-revolutionary disorder. Of course, it is not necessary or even mythically traditional for The Father to have no children of his own. Still, it does make him a particularly interesting historical example of an idealized father whose task is to contend with and overcome conceptual chaos. He was not the biological father of men, but a father of ideas and ideals and a man who was extremely conscious of the fact that he was setting the standards for both a country and the standards by which all of his predecessors would inevitably be measured.

Notable, too, is his reputation as the "American Cincinnatus." Washington ruled, but he never seized power and quickly relinquished it when he felt that his duty had ended. He refused a salary when he was appointed commander of the Continental Army, even though he had substantial debts and could barely afford to work without pay. Washington often experienced personal financial difficulty by leaving his estate in the hands of others while he took on public responsibilities. He didn't benefit financially from the duties for which he is best remembered. George Washington clearly wasn't motivated by greed or power or even immediate fame. His actions seem to have been motivated by order and righteousness, and his most selfish preoccupation seems to have been concerning his own long-term public honor and legacy.

In this time of unhinged reactionary hysteria accelerated by social media and partisan news entertainment, many men have looked to stoic philosophers as an antidote. Washington's peers and biographers regarded him as a master of emotional control who was proud of his poker face. As he once said, "With me it has always been a maxim rather to let my designs appear from my works than by my expressions."[86] Washington was not cold. He was passionate and thumotic. His ability to control his emotions and wait for the right time to say the right thing was a practice he imposed on himself and a skill that he developed with age and experience.

While Washington was often difficult to read and careful about what he revealed, he was tactical but not guileful or dishonest about his intentions. As Chernow observed, "There was cunning in Washington's nature but no low scheming. He never reneged on promises and was seldom duplicitous or underhanded. He respected the public, did not provoke people needlessly, and vowed at the time of his inauguration 'that no man shou[ld] ever charge me justly with deception.'"[87] Washington was good at being a man, but he was also a profoundly good man. As an exemplar, his story is an admirable retort to those nihilists who refer too often and lovingly to sociopathic and Machiavellian passages in books like *The 48 Laws of Power*.

Washington was not only a human example of The Father and The Striker — he was also a Lord of the Earth who was intensely interested in farming, animal husbandry, and land management. In his younger years, he was known for his enthusiastic involvement in the day-to-day work on his farms at Mount Vernon.

"Each day he rode twenty miles on horseback and personally supervised field work, fence construction, ditch drainage, tree planting, and dozens of other activities. An active presence,

he liked to demonstrate how things should be done, leading by
example. One startled visitor expressed amazement that the
master 'often works with his men himself, strips off his coat
and labors like a common man.'"[88]

Washington researched and experimented with a wide variety of crops and crop rotations and kept exceptionally detailed notes on his findings. He is even credited with the development of the American mule, also known as the American Mammoth Jackstock. Washington was interested in commerce, engaged in a substantial amount of land speculation, and campaigned tirelessly for a Potomac river canal system, which he had envisioned in the years between the Revolutionary War and his Presidency. He was deeply involved in shaping the world around him, and he made intentional and carefully considered choices about everything from the architecture of his home to the style of his clothing. Washington despised undisciplined drunkenness, but he drank wine, he was an avid theater-goer, and he loved to dance. As distant and idealistic as he could be, he was also quite worldly and still very much a man of the earth.

George Washington was a farmer, a soldier, and a leader. All men are endowed with differing aptitudes and potentials, certainly, but men can get too caught up in the idea of being one thing to the exclusion of all others. Washington ascended, guided by what he would have called Providence and aided by his own work and wisdom, to become an earthly paragon of The Father. But George Washington was multi-dimensional — he was a whole man, and he lived a whole life. His solar example shows how all of the eternal ideals of The Father, The Striker, and the Lord of the Earth can exist harmoniously together not only in society or in some conceptual system but also in the mind and in the life of one man.

SOLAR IDEALISM

"But the thing a man does practically believe (and this is often enough without asserting it even to himself, much less to others); the thing a man does practically lay to heart, and know for certain, concerning his vital relations to this mysterious Universe, and his duty and destiny there, that is in all cases the primary thing for him, and creatively determines all the rest. That is his religion; or, it may be, his mere skepticism and no-religion: the manner it is in which he feels himself to be spiritually related to the Unseen World or No-World; and I say, if you tell me what that is, you tell me to a very great extent what the man is, what the kind of things he will do is."

—Thomas Carlyle. *On Heroes, Hero-Worship & the Heroic in History* (1840)

SOLAR IDEALISM

90

To look upward and imagine a perfected ideal of man...that is not new.

To imagine — to know — that there is a better, more effective, more beautiful way to do everything that you are struggling to do in your everyday life... that is not new.

To recognize and elevate and revere excellence in yourself and in the men around you... that is not new.

To say that health is better than sickness, that strength is better than weakness, that courage is better than fear, that intelligence is better than stupidity, that competence is better than bumbling, that beauty is better than ugliness, that enterprise is better than laziness, that fortitude is better than fragility, that emotional control is better than unhinged hysteria, that plenty is preferable to scarcity, that self-determination is better than servility, that order is better than chaos...none of this is new and all of it is true. In fact, we could say without much fear of error that men have held these truths to be self-evident since the beginning of time.

Thousands or even hundreds of years ago, men had no need for what I am calling solar idealism - because they saw the sun rise every morning, and they knew that it was good. Because they saw the men around them who did the work that needed to be done better, and they recognized the men who did the best work, and they wanted to be more like them. Because they had fathers who provided for them and protected them and maintained order and taught them how to be men. Because it was natural for them to imagine a father who was better than any of their fathers, a leader who led their leaders, a higher king, a shining father of fathers who was stronger and more daring, whose life was everlasting, who saw more and knew more because he ruled from above and from the beginning.

No, they wouldn't have needed someone to say these things. And neither should you. The things that I am saying here should sound obvious and straightforward, and they are. You could play devil's advocate with the details of any given point, and you can find exceptions to every rule, and that can be a fun little game — to turn a thing on its head and look at it from a different angle. But, if you are being honest with yourself…I know that, as a man, you know that what I am saying is true. That's it's right. Because it is part of you, and I didn't make it up.

I don't care what name you call The Father or if you think it's just a story or an idea. It doesn't matter. I believe that the vast majority of men share a set of holy positives, a sacred sense of order that transcends variations in faith, philosophy, and cultural morality.

I don't care what religion you were raised with or what part of the world your people are from. You and I — we are men, and we worship excellence. And we always have. *Areté* is the light at the center of our holy order — our natural hierarchy.

The men who came before us didn't need to be reminded of this because it was understood. Of course a man should always want to be better at all of the things that he does and revere the ideal of what is best.

No...one...two...three...four hundred years ago, no average or man of accomplishment, anywhere, would ever have to say these things.

Every noble instinct in man beholds excellence and wants to reach toward it, to strive as best he can to at least approach it if not attain it, and it is his most noble — most virtuous — ambition to embody it.

There is a saying that a man should kill his idols. This doesn't mean that a man shouldn't have idols. It means that a man's goal should be to work so hard to emulate greatness that he himself becomes great. To become the man who raises the bar, who achieves more, and becomes the man who is emulated. Even in the most secular terms, man's noblest dream is apotheosis — to become the revered ideal, the north star for other men. This is the spur of the man who wants to break a record or plant his flag on some untouched peak or even planet. To boldly go, as it is said, where no man has gone before. To be the one out of many.

The noble, virtuous response to the witness of excellence is to be awed by it and to revere it, and if the pursuit of that particular excellence is in harmony with a man's own interests and talents, to then strive to emulate and reproduce that excellence with the ultimate aim of surpassing it. It is in this way that man best serves his soul and his nature, and if this excellence is deified — then his god within or beyond himself. Through this excellence and achievement, he raises the expectations of the men around him, and — ideally — they, too, become better.

Oh, this is old and simple stuff — "iron sharpens iron."

I can see a man do something well that I know I will never be able to do or even want to do myself, but I can still acknowledge and revere the righteousness of his achievement. I don't even have to like him personally to be able to do that. While I am hesitant to use the word enemy, it is a point of pride for me that I can still acknowledge excellence in men I believe to have wronged me. I believe that a healthy, masculine mind can say, "I don't like that guy, and he treated me poorly, and I will never trust him or support him or invest in him in any way, and I don't want him in my life or anywhere near me — but I have to admit that he is very good at this or that." One should be able to thoroughly dislike a man without having to belittle his legitimate achievements. Most of the best men I know can rise above pettiness in this way.

While the noble response to the witness of excellence is to be awed by it, to revere it, and ideally to emulate it, the ignoble and unmanly response to witnessing excellence is jealousy and the hatred of excellence. Ressentiment. This is also the easiest and laziest response. It is far easier to devalue excellence than it is to pursue it. It is far more comfortable to hate excellence than it is to acknowledge it as an ideal and revere it while also understanding that life is not and has never been fair and being honest enough with oneself to recognize one's own shortcomings and limitations. The less gifted or handicapped man with a healthy mind and upward-looking spirit will admit that it would be better to be more talented or more able-bodied, but will vow to work to be the best that he can be at whatever he is able and inclined to do. However, that mindset requires self-awareness and honesty and the acceptance of hard and unfair truths. It is much easier to complain about unfairness. If the deck has been stacked against you and you are being actively suppressed or prevented from pursuing excellence, there is nothing ignoble about fighting for self-determination. This is different from demanding support and affirmation for merely existing, insisting that excellence be redefined to comfort you and spare your feelings.

Unfortunately, this latter outlook is becoming the prevailing attitude of our age. The broken and the hurt and the ignoble want to revalue all values so that they feel affirmed and esteemed without having to improve themselves. If they are weak, they want to redefine strength. If they are fearful, they demand the redefinition of courage. If they are lazy, they say that industriousness is a value of some external oppressor and invent victimized rationales for why, like spoiled children, they should be given something for doing nothing. If they are ugly or obese, they want to redefine beauty. If they are emotionally unstable or prone to desperate oversharing or have never developed any self control whatsoever — they criticize men who have developed that control and project their own hysterical instability onto them. These adversaries of areté want the world remade in their own broken images not only because they are angry and jealous, but also because they are so externally focused that they cannot love themselves until they are universally affirmed and congratulated for being whatever they believe that they are.

These venomous, needy souls speak of "toxic masculinity," but who is more toxic than the person who needs to change to the whole world so that they can love themselves?

In an earlier age, this sickness would have been dismissed. But today, it is encouraged. Modern democratic institutions and their commercial partners have created a situation in which pandering to human weakness and encouraging dependence is far more profitable than promoting a culture of strength and personal sovereignty. There is more money and there are more votes to be gained by flattering people for doing nothing and faking sympathy for them and doling out cheap hits of dopamine than there ever will be for encouraging excellence. Excellence is naturally exclusive and somewhat elusive. If you want to sell potato chips and welfare checks, you appeal to the hoi polloi — the lowest common denominator.

In more tribal or nationalistic times, leaders invested in making their people stronger, because only the stronger tribes and nations would survive and prosper. The long-term success of the nation was the legacy of the leader. Today's globalist leaders have no true nations or people to empower. They are essentially free and fundamentally unprincipled power-seeking agents, and as such, they want the people they manage to be weak, dependent, and easily manipulated into compliance.

The natural, hierarchical values of vertically-oriented men are inconvenient for them. Fixed and unchanging values of any kind are inconvenient for them. So they undermine virtue cultures with clever value inversions and questions and a preference for exceptions over general rules. The formula of "well, this isn't always that..." is used to up the door to create a confusing environment in which everything can be anything, in which all definitions are written on a chalkboard, and every goalpost is movable.

The arguments for revaluation or the rewriting or expansion of values are always supported by maudlin entreaties for inclusiveness or fairness or freedom or empathy — offering the warm and buoyant bosom of comfort and acknowledgment to the unfortunate, unusual, overlooked, and disaffected. This, however, is merely the pitch, the sell — the appeal to emotion. The net effect is a total disorientation and destabilization of values, the extent of which I doubt even Nietzsche could have foreseen or imagined.

If there is no consistent agreement on what is "good," then the orienting axis of "good" can be moved at any time according to the fluctuating interests of those in power. If there is no "normal," a "new normal" can be manufactured at any time at the whim of oligarchs from behind the guarded gates of their decentralized Elysium.[89] When the "new normal" and the new "good" have been determined by elites and disseminated by propagandists, those who are ambitious but unprincipled will become "early adopters" and parrot the new values to seek the favor of those in power. Do you not see this happening all around you?

People can be pushed off guard and off balance by unlikely and contradictory questions. "What if vulnerability is strength? What about female masculinity? What if down is really up? Or what if there is no up or down and direction is an illusion? What if there are an infinite number of genders? What if slavery is freedom? What if good is evil? What if god is the devil? Wouldn't you love a meatless burger?"

When the barrage of contradictory combinations of ideas is nonstop and rapid-fire, what appears to be consensus reality starts to sound like a Charles Manson prison rant. Some have called this bizarre, constantly shifting mainstream consensus reality the "clown world," and many of us move through it in head-shaking, wide-eyed wonder — pointing and sputtering in this big tent full of shabby harlequins and dark comedy.

Our curse is that none of it makes sense, and we want it to make sense because it is in our nature to seek and create order. We have an ordered, hierarchical vision of the world and we assume that others are just confused, and that they want to create an ordered world with a hierarchy of values that makes sense to us, and that they are simply misled or doing it wrong or making mistakes. But, what if chaos and a world without fixed values or points of orientation and a return to the void is what people want, and what they're trying consciously or unconsciously to initiate through their feverish deconstructions? What if that is what is being planned and promoted for them?

Accept, for a moment, the possibility that people aren't actually interested in making sense or even trying to make sense, and that maybe they don't really care about what they claim to care about at all. Maybe they aren't being reasonable because they don't care about being reasonable. Because it's not a priority. Maybe most of them have given up, and are just riding the current...

It has been the fate and the work of men in every age to contend with some form of chaos, some swell of disorder that threatens to overtake them and catch them in its undertow. Sometimes that deluge is a plague, in others times, a famine, and quite often, a war. The challenge of our time is to reckon with this collapse of consensus, this conceptual chaos, this insidious deconstruction of hierarchy. Our struggle is the struggle of The Father in Darkness. Our ordeal is to make our way through a realm of madness, to make sense of the world, to find cosmic order in disarray, to draw and redraw the lines, to start a fire and follow its light out until it disappears into the void. To walk the line of that flickering perimeter and lay claim to the space within it. And if, to protect it, we must invoke the thundering Striker, let it be in the name of righteous order. Do not grab the hammer for blood or soil or coin or to set one name of The Father against another. It's too late for all of that now. We've come too far and seen too much. If the spear of Mars trembles, let it be not for the freedom to pursue happiness — that fickle distraction — but for the freedom to pursue excellence.

We are the First Men all over again. We come from everywhere and nowhere, but wherever we came from, we can never go back. We can only wander through this disordered and disorienting wilderness in and around and at the edges of the Empire of Nothing, looking for a spot to make our stand. To insist on order, to insist on excellence, to insist on strength and health and beauty and brilliance, to insist on virility and vitality and esteem virtuosity. To defiantly draw these lines in the dust of it all and keep them, even as the winds of dissolution blow and the sun sinks and definition blurs in the failing light. It is our job in the midst of all of this to build an upward-looking culture that inspires and elevates greatness in men and aims at a perfection above and beyond that which any man can attain.

It is up to us to be the men and see the gods.

It is up to us to put eagles back in our skies and in our hearts.

It is up to us to build something from almost nothing — to start the world we want because we can't wait for someone else to do it.

Like so many men who came before us, as the sun is setting, it is our job to build a fire in the dark.

AFTERWORD

In an age that enshrines "reality," in which one can become "famous" for being "real" by exposing one's worst and most mundane moments, my aim is to inspire men to rise above that and inspire other men by striving to show others their best.

Acknowledge the real, by all means — be a man of the Earth — but strive to embody the ideal. Have the courage to become the dream. Show the world not simply who you are, but who you want to be and what you believe is best.

While writing this book, a reader asked me how a man would live as a solar idealist. Because this book was intended for a broad audience, I prioritized the poetic over the practical in writing it. I believe that my job is to inspire, not direct. But I know that men of action or men who aspire to action want "action items." They want to know what I believe that they should do, and they want suggestions for how they might apply this philosophy in the context of their own lives.

As I mentioned in the preface, there will be readers who have already committed themselves to a religion, ideology, or identity, and those who are looking for some kind of "spiritual technology" that they can adopt as their own and incorporate into their identities. For those who are looking for rituals and methods of revering these eternal ideals, with the help of others, in the future, I will be developing and suggesting practices that relate to the tripartite system of integrated god-concepts presented in this book. I've already built a temple to "The Striker" and performed rituals invoking The Father at Waldgang, my sacred space. Since I began writing it, I have looked forward to creating and commissioning and hopefully inspiring the creation of works of art and cultural events that bring The Father, The Striker, and the Lord of the Earth to life in new and relevant forms. These ideals have been adopted and interpreted and revived by so many cultures before us. I see this effort not as the creation of "new gods" but as a new variation on the very oldest themes. So, there is much to do and more to come. However, within the context of this book, I'm going to offer some suggestions for ways in which I think the broadest range of men can take these ideas and run with them.

To "live" Solar Idealism is to elevate and revere a holistic and ultimately unattainable ideal of masculinity that transcends time and space and culture. To believe that it is the work of man is to imitate The Father, represented by the ever-present sun, by creating order in the midst of chaos. To understand that the protection and championing of that order will require the tactical virtues of Strength, Courage, Mastery, and Honor. To recognize that we are men of the Earth who will always be bound to it, men of flesh and blood who are tasked with taking control of the chaotic natural world and using its bounty to perpetuate order and life and create beauty, warmth and joyfulness for ourselves and the men and women and children within our circles. To "live" Solar Idealism is to profess a hierarchy of values guided by the light of that which is perfect while recognizing that the perfect is unattainable and refusing to make the perfect the enemy of the good. To "live" Solar Idealism is to commit oneself to the lifelong pursuit of manly excellence — of areté.

The best way to begin this pursuit is to read the myths and be inspired by them. No matter where you come from or what religion you profess, you'll never be poorer for having read the Greek myths or the *Enūma Eliš* or *The Rig Veda* or the Eddas. There are lessons in them for the kings and fathers and warriors and working men in all of us.

Read historical accounts of real-life heroes. Men of the hour who took action, men who were great leaders, men who were great craftsmen and artists and builders. Their stories will show you how it has been done, and remind you that when no one thought there was a way, some man made one.

Reading about gods and heroes is not worth much unless it inspires you to take action. Populate your mental and physical world with ideas and images related to your ideals, but take the next step and emulate those ideals. Challenge yourself. Push yourself to become more like those ideals in all areas of life and as often as possible. We cannot become our heroes. We revere them so that we can become better versions of ourselves.

Reject the corrosive tendency to dismiss the greatness of historical men by holding them accountable to contemporary morality. Julius Caesar was not subject to the Geneva Convention. George Washington had slaves. It is a grave, cowardly, and despicable error to defame men of the past and refusing to learn from or be inspired by their examples simply because they did things that would not currently be permissible or "politically correct."

Likewise, reject the tendency to defame living men according to the latest trending cause.

Reject the tendency to redefine eternal values or water them down to be more inclusive or accessible. High ideals are always exclusive and difficult to attain. They should be. Everyone cannot be a winner at everything, and certainly not without trying. The laws of supply and demand dictate that anything that everyone already is or has cannot have a high value. If everyone is equally good, then "goodness" has no value, and this applies to anything that could rightfully be called a virtue. Everyone may indeed be as special as a snowflake, but in light of this, being special or unique to that degree is not exceptional, but as common as common can be.

Elevate men who exhibit the values you admire. Do not fall prey to the jealous fear of acknowledging that a man does something better than you do or the fear of being regarded as a "fanboy." If you have your own merit, it will be evident. Give credit where it is due. There can be no pantheon if men refuse to elevate their heroes.

Abandon "sniping" culture. Sending out anonymous snark is not consistent with any masculine ideal. Making bitchy little comments is not consistent with any masculine ideal. And, further, rude little stick figure drawings do not "fight" degenerate culture. They are representative of a degenerate culture. Don't scribble on the walls of a brothel and call it a crusade. Do better.

For too long, men who believe in masculine virtue have stayed behind the scenes grumbling about the state of men and the state of the world. While they complained and polished their guns and played video games or chased money, they let women and the worst men — opportunistic men without integrity or values, even men who hate men and hate being men — run their institutions for them. The situation in which men find themselves is a direct result of this. If you want to live in a world that elevates masculine virtue, it is your job and your duty to step forward, get involved, and become a force of change. We can't all wait for the king beneath the mountain to return. That king...might be you.

Create groups with established hierarchies of values in which men can be formally recognized for their achievements. Give men a place to "level up" in real life, among their peers, instead of video games.

Build companies and educational institutions that unapologetically support, reward, and encourage excellence in men. This does not demand the denigration of women but simply acknowledges that men and women are different and supports the distinct path and the needs of men. In fact, one hopes that women who recognize the value of excellence in men could be enlisted to support such endeavors, as they have been through the ages.

Where are our Kiplings? Men today still quote the old poets while claiming to hate poetry. Perhaps we need some manly poets.

Create, commission, or purchase art and music and film that elevates masculine virtue and manly ideals. Throughout history, men have surrounded themselves with images and sounds that depicted and evoked excellence in men. They walked through streets and grand halls and temples and cathedrals that enshrined masculine virtue, and this lifted their spirits and inspired them to try harder and reach higher. For too long, men have ceded the ateliers of cultural creation to petulant men and the adversaries of manly virtue. I believe that it is almost impossible to overstate the extent to which that poisonous influence has contributed to the decline of men. It is not enough to point to the past and say, "see?" We cannot live in the past. Men in the past lived in their present, and they created a contemporary culture to inspire their contemporaries.

This list is short and incomplete. It is not an end, but a place to begin...

ACKNOWLEDGEMENTS

I discussed the ideas in this book with many men while I was writing it, but Clinton McMillan has been my constant collaborator and advisor in matters practical and arcane. I want to thank the men who stuck with me and kept coming back to Waldgang to participate in our evolving rituals because they recognized something powerful and eternal in what we've been doing. Nick, Michael, Gangin' Bob, and Nathan, among others. I'd also like to thank some of my early readers, including Tanner Guzy and some of my Patreon subscribers. And finally, I'd like to thank Lucio for his consistent support and for coming with me and being a constant presence in my life on this crazy ride through big cities and small towns and strange groups and changing ideas. People come and go in this life, and time sorts them out. The value of loyalty becomes more apparent with every passing year.

I would also like to thank The Father, The Striker, and the Lord of the Earth — as they exist in me, and existed before me. In my life, I've been able to see and do and say and create things that I don't think anyone would have been able to predict or expect from merely examining my relatively normal and humble beginnings. On paper, it's a hell of a story, and the math of it doesn't work out. I shouldn't have been the guy who wrote *The Way of Men*, but I was. I shouldn't be able to write this book, but I am. Sometimes I feel as though I've been pulling all of this down from somewhere else. While I've always been a skeptic, it seems to me that I've been guided along this path by what George Washington would have called "the hand of providence." I believe that, in my own way, I've been doing The Father's work.

ENDNOTES

1   Anthony Burgess. *The Wanting Seed*. 1962.

2   "Harrison Bergeron" is a short story written by Kurt Vonnegut in 1961. In the pursuit of social equality, anyone who is good at anything is "handicapped" by the state to remove their advantages. Good looking people are forced to wear masks or clown noses. Strong and athletic people are weighed down. TV announcing jobs are only given to people with speech impediments. Smart people are forced to wear distracting ear devices or headphones so that they have trouble thinking. It's a brilliant and extremely short story that, like the work of Orwell or Huxley, has become increasingly relevant with age. It can usually be found online and read for free.

3   Jung, C. G.. *The Red Book: A Reader's Edition: A Reader's Edition* (Philemon) (pp. 160-161). W. W. Norton & Company. Kindle Edition.

4   *Ibid. (p. 173)*.

5   Alternate translation: "One place there is called Hlidskjalf [Watchtower]. When Odin sat in its high seat, he could see through all worlds and into all men's doings. Moreover, he understood everything he saw."

Byock, Jesse L.. *The Prose Edda* (Penguin Classics) . Penguin Books Ltd. Kindle Edition.

6   Rough phonetic pronounciation : [HLEEDTHskyalv]. The "j" is pronounced like the "y" in "yes," and the accent over the "a" simply means that the "a" is a little longer, perhaps like an "ah."

7   Campbell, Joseph. The Inner Reaches of Outer Space: Myth As Metaphor and As Religion (The Collected Works of Joseph Campbell Book 10) (p. 27). Joseph Campbell Foundation. Kindle Edition.

8   A line from the Havamal (The Sayings of Har, or Odin) "Each word led

me on to another word...," a line spoken by Odin reflecting on his experience drinking the mead of poetry or inspiration.

9   Mallory, J.P. and Adams, D. Q.. *The Oxford Introduction to Proto-Indo-European and the Proto-Indo-European World*. 2006. p 114.

10   "By the erection of a fire altar, Agni is made present, and communication with the world of the gods is ensured; the space of the altar becomes a sacred space."

Mircea Eliade, *The Sacred and the Profane*. Harcourt. (p. 30)

11   Mallory, J.P. and Adams, D. Q.. *The Oxford Introduction to Proto-Indo-European and the Proto-Indo-European World*. 2006.

12   The Proto-Indo-European root of the word camp (*-kamp) means "to bend." As the word evolved in numerous languages, it came to mean an open field where military exercises and preparations were made, and sometimes a battlefield. Contemporary recreational campers promote the idea that campers should "leave no trace," but a military camp or a more semi-permanent camp without modern synthetic tents would make use of raw materials in the area and alter it. It is perhaps simply a coincidence that "to camp" once meant "to bend," but it is easy to imagine an association with men bending and breaking branches to create temporary shelters, which is exactly what modern bushcrafters would do in the absences of a tent. When men camp, they "bend" nature to their will.

13   For a deep dive on the meaning of the word hierós, see pp. 464-469 of Émile Benveniste's *Dictionary of Indo-European Concepts and Society*.

14   There are many methods and ideas associated with sacrifice, so I'll take a moment to explain the intent in this situation, so that I am not misunderstood. I have never intentionally performed a "scapegoat" sacrifice, and this was not a transactional sacrifice along the lines of killing a goat or a chicken to appease the anger of the gods or to ask them for good luck, or money, or the attention of a love interest. The point of this sacrifice was to re-enact the original sacrifice, the original act of creative destruction — in this case referencing the murder of Ymir and the creation of the world from his corpse. It was an alchemical act of transformation, meant to initiate a positive paradigm shift in all of the men present, and encouraging them to make the necessary sacrifices in their own lives to start their own worlds. I also think it's important for men to witness an animal die and to understand the gravity of that — to understand and appreciate that life comes from death and all creation necessitates some form of destruction.

In this cosmopolitan age of plenty and entitlement, people eat meat every day that comes from the store or a restaurant and never witness the death of an animal. I believe that this leads to profound misunderstandings about both the brutal nature of existence and the miracle of life, and it keeps men and women in a protected, passive, dependent, childlike state. Everyone who eats meat should watch an animal die at least once. This should never be done with cruelty or animosity — only with a somber sense of resignation and necessity. It's a powerful and emotional experience, and men who witness it in a ritual context carry that with them. After the sacrifice, we skin and butcher the animal, and I always try to use as much of it for food as possible and practical.

15 The meat of this ritual was eventually reworked into the essay, "The Joy of Thor," which is available online at https://www.jack-donovan.com/sowilo/2019/04/12/the-joy-of-thor/

16 The word jotnar means "devourers."

17 For a list of well-established "human universals," visit : https://condor. depaul.edu/~mfiddler/hyphen/humunivers.htm, or read the list in Pinker's *The Blank Slate* (2002), originally compiled by Donald E. Brown in *Human Universals* (1991).

18 For an in-depth look at the way Georges Dumézil distinguishes between the two aspects of Indo-European kingship in the Vedic, Germanic and Roman sources, see his book *Mitra-Varuna*.

19 Moore, Robert. *King, Warrior, Magician, Lover: Rediscovering the Archetypes of the Mature Masculine* (p. 156). HarperCollins. Kindle Edition.

20 There is no reference to Dumézil in *King, Warrior, Magician, Lover*, though Mircea Eliade was mentioned and recommended. Eliade was Dumézil's contemporary, they had met, and Dumézil praised Elaide's work, so there may be some first or second hand influence there.

21 Moore, Robert. *King, Warrior, Magician, Lover: Rediscovering the Archetypes of the Mature Masculine* (p. 49). HarperCollins. Kindle Edition.

22 *Ibid.* (p. 79).

23 *Ibid.*

24 *Ibid.* (p.99)

25 indle Edition.Plato. *The Republic*. In Book VI, (507b–509c)

26 "the original meaning of his name is unknown, but at one period of Egyptian history it seems to have been thought that the word rā indicated "operative and creative power," and that as a proper name it represented in meaning something like "Creator," this epithet being used much in the same way and with the same idea as we use the term when applied to God Almighty, the Creator of heaven and earth and of all things therein."

Budge, E. A. Wallis. *The Gods of the Egyptians, Volume 1* . Dover Publications. K

27 "The Virāj metre was the privilege of Mitra and Varuṇa; the Triṣṭubh metre was part of the day of Indra. The Jagatī entered into all the gods. That was the model for the human sages.

That was the model for the human sages, our fathers, when the primeval sacrifice was born. With the eye that is mind, in thought I see those who were the first to offer this sacrifice.

The ritual repetitions harmonized with the chants and with the metres; the seven divine sages harmonized with the original models. When the wise men looked back along the path of those who went before, they took up the reins like charioteers."

Doniger, W. (2005). *The Rig Veda*. Penguin UK.

28   Doniger, W. (2005). *The Rig Veda*. Penguin UK. (pp. 211-212).

29   In Indo-Iranian, the root of Mitra's name, *mitra, means "that which causes to bind."

30   Dumézil, Georges, and Derek Coltman. *Mitra-Varuna: An Essay on Two Indo-European Representations of Sovereignty*. 2nd ed., New York, Zone Books, 1988. (p. 72)

31   *Ibid.* Specifically, the chapters "Wodanaz and Tiwaz," and "The One-Eyed God and the One-Handed God."

32   'Tyr is the name of another of the Æsir. He is the boldest and most courageous, and it is very much up to him who wins in battle. For men of action, he is good to invoke."

Jesse L. Byock. *The Prose Edda* (Penguin Classics).

33   Homer, et al. *The Iliad*. Reissue, Penguin Classics, 1998. (427) Book 16, Lines 515-546.

34   This translation is mixed and simplified, based on the comparative work done here: http://web.archive.org/web/20120206205737/https://notendur. hi.is/haukurth/norse/reader/runatal.html

35   "Odin is the highest and oldest of the gods. He rules in all matters, and, although the other gods are powerful, all serve him as children do their father."

Jesse L. Byock. *The Prose Edda* (Penguin Classics).

36   Hesiod. *The Theogony, Works and Days, and The Shield of Heracles* (p. 31). Neeland Media LLC. Kindle Edition.

37   "Under this common-sense barbarian appreciation of worth or honour, the taking of life—the killing of formidable competitors, whether brute or human—is honourable in the highest degree. And this high office of slaughter, as an expression of the slayer's prepotence, casts a glamour of worth over every act of slaughter and over all the tools and accessories of the act."

Veblen, Thorstein. *Theory of the Leisure Class* (p. 13). Kindle Edition.

38   For an in-depth exploration of different thunderbolt symbols, read: Sibley, Jane. *The Divine Thunderbolt: Missile of the Gods*. Xlibris, 2009.

39   Heraclitus. *Fragments*. Number 28. "Τα πάντα δε οιακίζει κεραυνός."

Unsatisfied with the variations between English translations, I asked some native Greek readers, and their consensus was that the best translation would be "The Thunderbolt steers all things." κεραυνός is, of course, the thunderbolt associated with Zeus. Apparently, οιακίζω comes from a nautical root that means steering wheel, as in the wheel on a ship. Τα πάντα means "everything/all" and δε means "therefore/as a result."

40   "He launched two eagles soaring high from a mountain ridge
and down they glided, borne on the wind's draft a moment,
wing to wingtip, pinions straining taut till just
above the assembly's throbbing hum they whirled,
suddenly, wings thrashing, wild onslaught of wings
and banking down at the crowd's heads—a glaring, fatal sign—
talons slashing at each other, tearing cheeks and throats
they swooped away on the right through homes and city.
All were dumbstruck, watching the eagles trail from sight,
people brooding, deeply, what might come to pass..."

Homer, et al. *The Iliad*. Reissue, Penguin Classics, 1998. (Book 2, 164-174)
41   *Ibid.* (Book 20, 270.)
42   Doniger, W. (2005). *The Rig Veda*. Penguin UK. pp. 129. (4.26-7, "Soma and Indra and the Eagle."
43   Benveniste, Émile, and Elizabeth Palmer. *Dictionary of Indo-European Concepts and Society*. 1st ed., HAU, 2016. (p. 233)
44   Anthony, David. *The Horse, the Wheel, and Language: How Bronze-Age Riders from the Eurasian Steppes Shaped the Modern World*. Reprint, Princeton University Press, 2010.
45   *Ibid.* (p. 135)
46   "the lord of men Agamemnon sacrificed a fat rich ox,
five years old, to the son of mighty Cronus, Zeus,
and called the chiefs of all the Argive forces..."

Homer, Robert Fagles, et al. *The Iliad*. Reissue, Penguin Classics, 1998. (Book 2: 478)
47   Puhvel, Jaan. *Comparative Mythology*. The Johns Hopkins University Press, 1989. (Ch. 6)
48   ᚾ - Ur

"The aurochs is proud and has great horns;
it is a very savage beast and fights with its horns;
a great ranger of the moors, it is a creature of mettle."

- Anglo-Saxon Rune Poem, Dickens translation.

49   Jaan Puhvel, *Comparative Mythology*. (pp. 222-237).

50   Mallory, J., and D. Adams. *The Oxford Introduction to Proto-Indo-European and the Proto-Indo-European World (Oxford Linguistics)*. 1st ed., Oxford University Press, 2006. (pp. 436-437)

51   Kurcina, Michael. *We Fight Monsters: Wisdom and Inspiration That Speak to the Warrior's Soul*. Independently published, 2020.

52   Xenophon. *Conversations of Socrates (Classics)* (pp. 107-108). Penguin Books Ltd. Kindle Edition.

53   Mansfield, Harvey. *Manliness*. Yale University Press, 2007. (pp. 85)

54   *Ibid.* (pp. 206-207)

55   Anonymous. The Homeric Hymns and Homerica with an English Translation by Hugh G. Evelyn-White. *Homeric Hymns*. Cambridge, MA.,Harvard University Press; London, William Heinemann Ltd. 1914.

Alternate translation of "King of Manliness":

"You are a tyrant to the rebellious, a leader to the most just, *you carry the staff of manhood,* you whirl your disc of bright fire across the sky among the seven tracks of the constellations where blazing horses bear you forever beyond the third orbit."

Homer. *The Homeric Hymns* (Penguin Classics) (p. 133). Penguin Books Ltd. Kindle Edition.

56   Virgil, Robert Fagles, et al. *The Aeneid* (Penguin Classics Deluxe Edition). Reprint, Penguin Classics, 2008. (7. 685-715).

57   Eliade, Mircea, et al. *Rites and Symbols of Initiation: The Mysteries of Birth and Rebirth*. Spring Publications, 2017. See Chapter 2.

58   Turner, Victor. *The Ritual Process (Lewis Henry Morgan Lectures)*. 1st ed., Routledge, 1996. Chapter 3.

59   Again, for more, see *Rites and Symbols of Initiation: The Mysteries of Birth and Rebirth*.

60   Carson, Ciaran. *The Tain (Penguin Classics)*. Original, Penguin Classics, 2009. (pp. 37-38).

61   In *Comparative Mythology*, Jaan Puhvel makes this connection, describing Rudra as "the god of the wild, of chaos before cosmos, of nature antedating culture, of all that as yet, or ever, eludes control."

Puhvel, Jaan. *Comparative Mythology*. The Johns Hopkins University Press, 1989. (p. 58)

62   Anonymous, and Ralph Griffith. *The Rig Veda: Complete (Illustrated)*. Illustrated, CreateSpace Independent Publishing Platform, 2017. (Book 2, Hymn 34, Line 1).

63   *Ibid.* (Book 1, Hymn 85, Line 8).

64   "The Arii, fierce beyond the superiority of strength they possess over the other just enumerated people, improve their natural ferocity of aspect by artificial helps. Their shields are black; their bodies painted: they choose the darkest nights for an attack; and strike terror by the funereal gloom of their sable bands—no enemy being able to sustain their singular, and, as it were, infernal appearance; since in every combat the eyes are the first part subdued."

Tacitus, Cornelius. *The Agricola and The Germania* (p. 59). Neeland Media LLC. Kindle Edition.

65   I put skulls on the covers of *The Way of Men*, *Becoming a Barbarian*, and *A More Complete Beast* for both this reason, and because skulls are a universal symbol understood by all men. I knew that skull imagery would appeal to the kind of men who had recognized or were in the process of recognizing that an essential part of masculinity was cultivating the potential for violent action.

66   Mallory, J., and D. Adams. *The Oxford Introduction to Proto-Indo-European and the Proto-Indo-European World (Oxford Linguistics)*. 1st ed., Oxford University Press, 2006. (p. 433)

67   Jaan Puhvel observed in his *Comparative Mythology* that this tension between the potential berserker and the protective champion of law and order has always been implied in Indo-European myth, noting that:

"Those trained as agents of aggression and repression may experience difficulty functioning as normal human beings under great stress, or conversely when the pressure is off. Such abnormality also induces clannishness vis-à-vis the general society, "fraternal" orders, "protective" associations, gangs, juntas, and other forms of structured apartness." Puhvel, Jaan. *Comparative Mythology*. The Johns Hopkins University Press, 1989. (p. 241).

68   Mallory, J., and D. Adams. *The Oxford Introduction to Proto-Indo-European and the Proto-Indo-European World (Oxford Linguistics)*. 1st ed., Oxford University Press, 2006. (p. 434).

69   *Ibid.* (p. 166).

70   *Ibid.* (p. 255, 257).

71   Puhvel, Jaan. *Comparative Mythology*. The Johns Hopkins University Press, 1989. (p. 63).

72   Benveniste, Émile, and Elizabeth Palmer. *Dictionary of Indo-European Concepts and Society*. 1st ed., HAU, 2016. (p. 234).

73   *Ibid.* (pp. 236-237).

74   Puhvel, Jaan. *Comparative Mythology*. The Johns Hopkins University Press, 1989. (p. 150).

75   *Ibid.* (p. 169).

76   Cunliffe, Barry. *The Ancient Celts*. 2nd ed., Oxford University Press, 2018. (p. 275)

77   "Start The World Episode #29 - Dr. Mathias Nordvig on Heathenry and Norse Mythology." YouTube, uploaded by Jack Donovan, 6 July 2020, www.youtube.com/watch?v=OA-OKhMnxuw.

78   Byock, Jesse L.. *The Prose Edda* (Penguin Classics). Penguin Books Ltd. Kindle Edition.

79   Maslow, A. H.. *A Theory of Human Motivation* (p. 15). Start Publishing LLC. Kindle Edition.

80   Homer, Nicholas Richardson, et al. *Homeric Hymns* (Penguin Classics). 4th Printing, Penguin Classics, 2003. (p. 100)

81   Both areté and áristos come ultimately from the Proto-Indo-European root *h₂er-, which means "to fit, fix, or put together." This root also produces the Latin "ordo" (order) and the Sanskrit Ṛta ऋत, indicating a cosmic order, rule, or truth.

82   Jaeger, Werner, and Gilbert Highet. *Paideia: The Ideals of Greek Culture Volume I: Archaic Greece: The Mind of Athens*. 2nd ed., Oxford University Press, U.S.A., 1986. (p. 5).

83   Xenophon. *Conversations of Socrates* (Classics) (pp. 107-108). Penguin Books Ltd. Kindle Edition.

84   Kerényi, Carl, and Ralph Manheim. *Dionysos: Archetypal Image of Indestructible Life*. Princeton University Press, 1996.

85   "The administrative machinery of the Aryans in the Rig Vedic period functioned with the tribal chief, for his successful leadership in war, at the centre. He was called rajan. It seems that in the Rig Vedic period, the king's post had become hereditary. However, the rajan was a kind of chief and did not exercise unlimited power, having to reckon with the tribal organizations. We have traces of the election of the king by the tribal assembly called the samiti. The king was called the protector of his tribe. He protected its cattle, fought its wars, and offered prayers to the gods on its behalf."

Sharma, R.S.. *India's Ancient Past* (Kindle Locations 2282-2287). OUP India. Kindle Edition.

Note: The third sentence here seems to contradict the rest, but I've seen this idea repeated by others elsewhere throughout my studies. A lot of this is speculative, but I thought this was interesting enough to include.

86   Chernow, Ron. *Washington: A Life*. Penguin Publishing Group. Kindle Edition.

87   *Ibid.* (p. 605).

88   *Ibid.* (p.119).

89   See the film Elysium (2013). The film seems increasingly prophetic, as the gap between those with unimaginable wealth and those with nothing expands, and the middle class is actively attacked and undermined. Though

people cry "communism" and "fascism," it seems clear that the wealthy have no interest in seeing their wealth redistributed, and they have no attachment whatsoever to blood or soil. They seem to be creating a massive underclass that will be managed and exploited and perhaps sporadically culled by a floating aristocracy and a managerial class.

EXTRAS

MYTHIC TIMELINES

Non Indo-European

The Epic of Gilgamesh (Mesopotamia)	1800 BC
The Book of the Dead (Egypt)	1550 BC
Hebrew Bible	800-100 BC

Indo-European

Proto-Indo-European, the hypothetical root tongue of the Indo-European languages, is believed to have been spoken between 4500 and 2500 BC.

The Rig Veda (India)	1500 BC – 1200 BC
Homer - *Iliad, The Odyssey* (Greece)	1260–1180 BC
Hesiod - *Theogony*	730–700 BC
Apollonius Rhodius - *Argonautica*	200-300 BC
Pseudo-Apollodorus - *Bibliotheca*	1-100 BC
Virgil - *The Aeneid* (Rome)	19 BC
Beowulf (Old English)	975-1025 AD
Táin Bó Cúailnge (Ireland)	Set in 1-100 AD[1]
Prose, Poetic *Eddas* (Iceland)	1220-1300[2]

---

1   Manuscripts from 1001–1200 AD and later.

2   Set earlier

BIBLIOGRAPHY AND FURTHER READING

The translations or editions listed are the books I've read or had on hand — not necessarily the "best" or most complete translations. In cases where I have owned or referred to several translations and editions, in the list below, I selected the Penguin editions, for the sake of some conformity.

General Comparative Mythology

Eliade, Mircea, and Willard Trask. *The Sacred and The Profane: The Nature of Religion*. Harcourt Brace Jovanovich, 1987.

Eliade, Mircea, et al. *Rites and Symbols of Initiation: The Mysteries of Birth and Rebirth*. Spring Publications, 2017.

Turner, Victor. *The Ritual Process* (Lewis Henry Morgan Lectures). 1st ed., Routledge, 1996.

Campbell, Joseph. *The Hero with a Thousand Faces* (*The Collected Works of Joseph Campbell*). Third, New World Library, 2008.

Indo-European Studies

Anthony, David. *The Horse, the Wheel, and Language: How Bronze-Age Riders from the Eurasian Steppes Shaped the Modern World.* Reprint, Princeton University Press, 2010.

Dumézil, Georges, and Derek Coltman. *Mitra-Varuna: An Essay on Two Indo-European Representations of Sovereignty.* Reprint, Zone Books, 1990.

Puhvel, Jaan. *Comparative Mythology.* The Johns Hopkins University Press, 1989.

Mallory, J., and D. Adams. *The Oxford Introduction to Proto-Indo-European and the Proto-Indo-European World (Oxford Linguistics).* 1st ed., Oxford University Press, 2006.

Benveniste, Émile, and Elizabeth Palmer. *Dictionary of Indo-European Concepts and Society.* 1st ed., HAU, 2016.

Kershaw, Kris. *The One-Eyed God: Odin and the (Indo-) Germanic Männerbünde (Journal of Indo-European Studies Monograph No. 36).* Institute for the Study of Man, 2020.

Cunliffe, Barry. *The Ancient Celts.* 2nd ed., Oxford University Press, 2018.

Mythic Canon

George, Andrew. *The Epic of Gilgamesh* (Penguin Classics). 31732nd ed., Penguin Classics, 2003.

Anonymous, and Wendy Doniger. *The Rig Veda* (Penguin Classics). Penguin Classics, 2005.

  (This edition is a collection of excerpts, and serves as a brief and easily readable introduction to the main gods and concepts. For an English translation of the complete Rig Veda, see the edition below.)

Anonymous, and Ralph Griffith. *The Rig Veda: Complete (Illustrated)*. Illustrated, CreateSpace Independent Publishing Platform, 2017.

Hesiod, and M. West. *Theogony and Works and Days (Oxford World's Classics)*. Reissue, Oxford University Press, 2009.

Apollodorus, and Robin Hard. *The Library of Greek Mythology (Oxford World's Classics)*. 1st ed., Oxford University Press, 2008.

Homer, Nicholas Richardson, et al. *Homeric Hymns (Penguin Classics)*. 4th Printing, Penguin Classics, 2003.

Homer, Robert Fagles, et al. *The Iliad*. Reissue, Penguin Classics, 1998.

--- *The Odyssey*. Reprint, Penguin Classics, 1999.

Rhodes, Apollonius Of, and E. Rieu. *The Voyage of Argo: The Argonautica (Penguin Classics)*. 2nd ed., Penguin Classics, 1959.

Virgil, et al. *The Aeneid (Penguin Classics Deluxe Edition)*. Reprint, Penguin Classics, 2008.

Ovid, et al. *Metamorphoses (Penguin Classics)*. Reprint, Penguin Classics, 2004.

Carson, Ciaran. *The Tain (Penguin Classics)*. Original, Penguin Classics, 2009.

Heaney, Seamus. *Beowulf: A New Verse Translation*. Bilingual, Farrar, Straus and Giroux, 2000.

Hollander, Lee. *The Poetic Edda*. Revised, University of Texas

Press, 1962.

Sturluson, Snorri, and Jesse Byock. *The Prose Edda: Norse Mythology (Penguin Classics)*. 1st ed., Penguin Classics, 2006.

Grammaticus, Saxo, et al. *Saxo Grammaticus: The History of the Danes, Books I-IX: I.* English Text; II. Commentary (Bks.1-9). Revised, BOYE6, 1979.

Byock, Jesse, and Anonymous. *The Saga of the Volsungs (Penguin Classics)*. Unknown, Penguin Classics, 2000.

Philosophy

Heraclitus, et al. *Fragments (Penguin Classics)* (English and Greek Edition). Bilingual, Penguin Classics, 2003.

Plato, and Benjamin Jowett. *Symposium and Phaedrus*. Dover Thrift Editions, 1993.

Bloom, Allan, and Adam Kirsch. *The Republic of Plato*. 3rd ed., Basic Books, 2016.

Nietzsche, Friedrich, et al. *On the Genealogy of Morals (Penguin Classics)*. Reprint, Penguin Classics, 2014.

Nietzsche, Friedrich. *Beyond Good and Evil (Penguin Classics)* (Rev Ed) (1/28/03). Penguin Classics, Penguin Classics, 2003.

Nietzsche, Friedrich, Michael Tanner, et al. *The Birth of Tragedy: Out of the Spirit of Music (Penguin Classics)*. Unknown, Penguin Classics, 1994.

Nietzsche, Friedrich, and R. Hollingdale. *Thus Spoke Zarathustra: A Book for Everyone and No One (Penguin Classics)*. Penguin Classics, 1961.

Men's Studies

Moore, Robert, and Douglas Gillette. *King, Warrior, Magician, Lover: Rediscovering the Archetypes of the Mature Masculine.* Reprint, HarperOne, 1991.

Michler, Ryan. *Sovereignty: The Battle for the Hearts and Minds of Men.* Lifestyle Entrepreneurs Press, 2018.

Kurcina, Michael. *We Fight Monsters: Wisdom and Inspiration That Speak to the Warrior's Soul.* Independently published, 2020.

Miscellany

Chernow, Ron. *Washington: A Life.* Penguin Books, 2011.

Jaeger, Werner, and Gilbert Highet. *Paideia: The Ideals of Greek Culture Volume I: Archaic Greece: The Mind of Athens.* 2nd ed., Oxford University Press, U.S.A., 1986.

A SKY WITHOUT GODDESSES

1

It may seem conspicuous to some that this book includes no goddesses.

The Greeks, Romans, Celts and Germanic peoples all worshipped goddesses to some extent. Indeed, especially in the case of the Greeks, female gods were involved in legendary warfare. The bright-eyed Athena besting the man-slaughtering Ares — and fighting alongside Odysseus — in the works of Homer.

> "Athena, looming out of the rafters high above them,
> brandished her man-destroying shield of thunder, terrifying
> the suitors out of their minds, and down the hall they panicked"
>
> — Homer. The Odyssey. As translated by Robert Fagles

Greek society itself, like all of the Indo-European societies and all known civilizations*, was patriarchal in practice. While female gods interacted freely with male gods and heroes as peers, Athenian women were separated from men, were not considered citizens, and were not well-educated. They were not trained in warfare and they did not fight in wars. There is some evidence to support a minority of armed fighting Scythian-Sarmatian women, who may have inspired the tales of Amazons. However, the Sythians from the Eurasian steppe, while linguistically Indo-European, were hardly Greeks. These fighting women, to whatever extent they existed at all, were exotic foreigners.

So, while female gods took on male roles in the Greek sky, this was not the situation on the ground. Perhaps this shows that the abstract ideas that the gods represented were more important than the idea of gods as anthropomorphic beings. It is possible that reverence for female gods also introduced an element of balance to the male psyche in a male-dominated society. And whereas the monotheistic texts featured a single message from god that caused conflict and drama between humans, the polytheistic lore also included conflict and drama between the gods. So maybe female deities were needed to fill out the casts of the epics and eddas. For whatever reason, the worship of female gods and spirits by men is a phenomenon that has always been a perennial feature of paganism in patriarchal societies.

We no longer live in a patriarchal society. Males are expected to compete with females in school and in the workplace. Young males are for the most part taught by female teachers in schools that cater to female interests and indoctrinate them with radical feminist worldviews. The entertainment industry hypes female heroes as superior rivals to their male counterparts in everything from cops shows to superhero movies. In many cases, females have been cast as replacements for male icons.

Men don't need female gods or heroes, because they live in a world in which mainstream society elevates women in every aspect of public life. If a man wants to idealize an "amazing" woman, he can watch the latest flick featuring a woman in the role of Thor or 007. He can rent *Captain Marvel*.

The elevation of some idealized female in a spiritual context would only compound the mainstream narrative which pretends that men and women are the same — and, if anything, women are a little bit better. A man's home used to be his castle, but we live in an age when men are expected grovel to their wives for "man caves" — sad and cartoonish redoubts for their embattled male identities. Far too many men seek out a woman to mother them and treat them like naughty little boys who have to ask their wives or girlfriends for "permission" to spend unsupervised time with other men or to do things that might be "dangerous." In this kind of social context, revering a woman religiously seems laughably redundant.

Men who want to become better men and better at being men don't need another women to look up to. If you worship women in the 21st Century, you deserve to be enslaved by one.

There is a popular notion, which seems to have been popularized by Carl Jung and his supporters, that all men have a "feminine side" that they need to "get in touch with." This may have seemed novel or perhaps even necessary in a patriarchal society — but, again, we no longer live in one. When the influence of women is stiflingly ubiquitous in a man's outer world, the last thing he needs to do is spend time trying to enshrine some inner "feminine" self. Men today don't need to get in touch with their feminine "sides"—they need to get in touch with their masculine "sides."

This idea that we have some sort of bifurcated masculine/feminine system is not grounded in physical reality. There is no "masculine side" or "feminine side" — strictly speaking. Like myth, this is a frame that helps people order reality in a particular way to help them understand aspects of themselves and the world around them. Religions and ideologies and trends in psychology come and go based on how relevant and useful they are to a given community at a given time. The world has changed dramatically since this idea was popularized, and this "masculine side/feminine side" frame is no longer a helpful or positive model for men. If anything, it makes men weaker and more dependent.

When I search my soul, with all honesty, I must admit that every aspect of myself that I could associate with femininity could also be described accurately as a failure or lack of masculinity. I have no personal gnosis of the feminine experience. The feminine is something external, someone else's experience that I can only imagine and analyze from outside of it. I would not, and cannot, know what it is to be a woman or to feel like a woman. I can only recognize evidence of different behaviors and what I perceive to be different interests in men and women. I can identify feelings and behaviors that are woman-like. Our bodies shape our minds and our minds are part of our bodies, and, in some sense, inseparable from them. If I could upload my existing consciousness into a computer, all of its characteristics up to that moment would have been shaped by my experience of having a body - a male body with male hormones, who interacted with the external world as a male.

Men are men. They are completely men, and at a chromosomal level they were always going to be men. Men can't be anything but men. And to show them how to be better men — to point the way and inspire them to tap into their true potential as men — they need male role models and ideals and heroes. This is true more now than ever, precisely because there is no broad patriarchal social framework that advances masculine ideals. Masculine idealism was once held up publicly, but until it is again, men will have to make the extra effort to incorporate masculine ideals into their private worlds and their inner spiritual work.

The tripartite system of gods that I have presented in this book is a system of gods for men. It should be noted that these three types of gods were also generally the three most important and widely revered gods in the pantheons of the patriarchal systems form which they were drawn.

However, this system is only half of the bigger picture.

The sky god always mates with the chthonic earth mother.

Just as men need chaos to become men, they need women to produce more men. And I think healthy young men also need to have a healthy female influences in their lives, so that they don't develop foolish or unfairly skewed ideas about women.

Women are obviously part of the human experience. Individual women cannot be held accountable for the errors and excesses of feminism any more than the average citizen can be held responsible for the actions of his or her government. Today's women were born into a feminist system and they're just trying to figure life out and make the best of their situation.

Men and women are fundamentally different and they perceive reality in a different way. They have different orientations and interests. I believe that males should elevate male ideals and heroes and gods, and I encourage women to find feminine role models and exemplars and godesses.

2

Men often ask me what to look for in a woman, and over the years I have heard from many women who decided to read *The Way of Men* in an effort to better understand their husbands or boyfriends. So, instead of completely kicking the can down the road, I'll offer some of my thoughts on what it might mean to be a "solar woman."

Women who appreciate the values of masculine men have a tendency to try to please men by imitating them and trying to become one of the boys. Likewise, in a busy modern world, men get the idea that they should look for a woman who they can "bro" out with — who is or seems to be interested in all of the things that interest men. Sometimes unusually strong women seek out an even stronger man who makes them feel feminine — and I've seen this play out with female "strongmen" and bodybuilders and other athletes. Sometimes this works out and people find a balance, and sometimes they don't.

I don't think masculinizing women to make them bros is a solution that scales. A woman can never really be "one of the guys," no matter how much she wants to be or how much you want her to be. To other guys, she's always going to be your girlfriend/wife — not a "bro." Inserting her into every male group situation robs you and your friends of the social experience of the all-male group that most men so desperately need to establish and maintain their own independent sense of identity as men. A "solar woman" isn't a woman who tries to compete with men or push her way into every male group. And I think it's both unnatural and unfair to expect a "good woman" to try to become something she can never truly be. As with men, women should strive to become what they are and realize their own potential on their own terms.

Feminism did a great disservice to women by demanding an equality of apples and oranges and encouraging women to adopt the values and mimic the behaviors of men. It's absurd to suggest a woman isn't good enough unless she does the same work or makes as much money as a man. This presupposes that she has no separate and distinct value, which is its own kind of internalized misogyny.

Feminism "liberated" female sexuality, but it also commodified and devalued and female sexuality in the sexual marketplace. Feminism increased the amount of sex available to men and decreased the value of maintaining a monogamous or even consistent long-term sexual relationship with any given woman. And, in the current culture that promotes divorce, socially rewards any self-proclaimed victim, and encourages accusations of "misconduct" according to constantly changing standards of sexual and domestic etiquette — feminism has substantially increased the risk of any man who wants to invest in a relationship with a woman.

When men in the pre-feminist age looked for a wife, they weren't just looking for someone to have sex with. They were looking for a partner. They were looking for someone who shared their values, who would work with them to build a household and a family and take an active role in raising and educating their children. Men were looking for something different in women than what they looked for in their male friends. They were looking for a harmonious complement that enriched their lives — not a mirror. Before feminism, men were looking for women who wanted the same kind of life that they did, who wanted to move in the same direction and play an important and necessary but totally different role on the same team. When men and women can't agree on that role or that direction, when they don't want to build a family or a life together, when they don't share the same goals or values or have much in common...what is left between men and women but sex? Men don't need female "buddies." In its attempt to "liberate" female sexuality, feminism actually sexually objectified women by reducing what they had to offer to men aside from sex. Tinder and hook-up culture are also direct results of feminist "liberation," and have created an environment where men and women both feel used and very often end up alone, unhappy, and unfulfilled.

While I believe that women are closer to the earth and to nature and even to chaos — like the Lord of the Earth — I also believe that they are capable of looking upward and developing their own excellences and working with men to create and perpetuate order. In fact, for much of human history, that is exactly what most women have done. Men and women — while remaining different and taking different roles — were on the same team. They shared the same higher values and worked to perpetuate the same orders together.

So, to solar men who are looking for solar women — and to

women who want to know how to be a solar woman…

A solar woman either had a strong father and respects him, or didn't, but believes that men and fathers should be strong, and wants a strong father for her children if she has any.

A solar woman doesn't try to impress men by trying to be "one of the guys."

A solar woman knows and understands that men and women are different, and that men need their own space to become the best versions of what they are.

A solar woman is confident in her own value as a woman, and works to develop her own talents and excellences. She, too, seeks perfection and pushes toward the ideal in whatever she does.

A solar woman wants men to be masculine, and while she is neither cruel nor vulgar, she finds it disappointing and uninspiring when men are not masculine.

A solar woman holds men to the same standards and expects the same things from men that the best men want and demand from each other.

A solar woman recognizes the value of order, and respects the role men play in creating, protecting, and perpetuating order. She knows that she also has a role to play in the fight against chaos and the subversion of meaning, structure, and value, and she works together with men to create, protect, and perpetuate order.

Ultimately, if you're seeking a female partner, as with any cooperative enterprise — the two of you need to agree on the mission of the venture and the product and culture that you're aiming to produce. Like The First Men, a man and a woman must agree on a place to begin — a point of reference, an axis of values, a place that you can both look for and return when you've wandered too far out into the wilderness.

As the camp grows, men and women find each other and build their own fires together, expanding the range and power of the mandala as they place new points of light within the solar orbit of that central fire in the dark.

_____

*   The use of the word "civilization" is intentional here. While there is rare evidence of an occasional matriarchal tribe or subculture — no dominant civilization known to the historical record has been functionally matriarchal. Matrilineal, yes. Occasionally elevating Queens and Empresses as ruling figureheads, yes. A society where the majority of women officially rule households and dominate political decision-making? No. Much has been made of the supposed "equality" of women in the Viking Age, for instance, but upon a closer look at the source material, this appears to be for the most part modern political propaganda and wishful thinking.

In 2019, I started promoting a slogan that caught on, and in response to a lot of questions about what it meant to "stay solar," I sketched out an essay about it that I published online. Much of this material was later repeated throughout this book, but I've decided to include it in print here as an extra. They say that when you put something online it is "forever," and maybe in some sense that is true. But when hosting bills stop being paid and servers go offline, I have books that will be sitting in libraries and on bookshelves around the world long after I'm dead. Print matters.

STAY SOLAR

Throughout human history, and certainly, in Indo-European cultures, men have revered some force in the sky, associated with day and the light. The sky fathers and all-fathers reigned from above, and men looked upward to these primal patriarchs for guidance on how to live more righteously — how to take the higher path. As it is explained in Plato's *Republic*, this highest force and greatest good isn't quite the sun, but the sun is perhaps the best way to understand it — the sun is "the child of the good."

> "Now, that which imparts truth to the known and the power of knowing to the knower is what I would have you term the idea of good, and this you will deem to be the cause of science, and of truth in so far as the latter becomes the subject of knowledge; beautiful too, as are both truth and knowledge, you will be right in esteeming this other nature as more beautiful than either; and, as in the previous instance, light and sight may be truly said to be like the sun, and yet not to be the sun, so in this other sphere, science and truth may be deemed to be like the good, but not the good; the good has a place of honor yet higher."

> — Plato. The Republic

In true, complete darkness, there is no truth or beauty

whatsoever. True darkness is the void, and all things — all forms — are unintelligible. As Socrates makes clear, unlike the other sense organs, the eye requires light to see anything at all.

My formulation of what it means to stay or to be solar is a synthesis of mythic and scientific understandings of the sun and the nature of the cosmos. To our ancient ancestors, the sun made its way across the sky and disappeared at night, giving a sense to some that it was forced to "endure" the darkness and the night, only to emerge triumphant each morning. Today we know that the earth actually revolves around the sun, though the sun has its own very long orbit around the galaxy. Science tells us more than the ancients knew about gravity and space and the fiery nature of the sun, but to my mind, this information only enhances and adds depth to the analogies and metaphors about the sun and its influence over us.

While the solar mindset is present and even articulated in many religions, I don't believe it favors any particular one or conflicts with most of them. In fact, while the specific doctrines and elements of many religions may contain anti-solar elements that are servile and submissive or based in the dark jealousy of ressentiment, I believe that the qualities I am associating with the sun and solarity are consistent with the way most men envision a benevolent god or sovereign.

> *"...the thing a man does practically believe (and this is often enough without asserting it even to himself, much less to others); the thing a man does practically lay to heart, and know for certain, concerning his vital relations to this mysterious Universe, and his duty and destiny there, that is in all cases the primary thing for him, and creatively determines all the rest. That is his religion..."*

> — *Thomas Carlyle. On Heroes and Hero Worship and the Heroic in History.*

Many have asked me if "Stay Solar" is some kind of Stoic mantra. What "staying solar" has in common with Stoicism is emotional control, and as "life is conflict," maintaining emotional control is a challenge that ends only after death.

A lot of men talk about Stoicism without having read the Stoics. In the popular mind, Stoicism sometimes appears to mean "THIS IS SPARTA!!" or "suck it up" or "can't hurt me" and lends itself to a lot of tryhard tough-guy posturing. This would probably confuse a sensitive, thoughtful fellow like Marcus Aurelius, who, as far as I can gather, was not very much like Leonidas at all.

My beef with Stoicism is that it seems a bit too focused on acceptance, a bit too detached from outcomes...a bit too, "this is fine..."

The sun is hot and violent, made of fire and storm — but it retains its shape, its path, its gravity, and the system of order that spins around it.

GRAVITY

Know your purpose. Stay centered and on task. Aim, whenever possible, to be an unmoved mover — to be a cause rather than an effect or the affected. Do not allow yourself to be pulled into petty disputes or frivolous pursuits. Remember who you are and what you are doing, and what your responsibilities are — and for all of it, why. Know your reasons and motivations — cultivate self-awareness.

One could call this "discipline," but something about the word discipline sounds like a cracking whip to my ear — though it comes from the same root as "disciple" and implies the acceptance of teaching or an external order.

Perhaps it is more productive and life-affirming to think about maintaining a clarity of identity and purpose and evaluating patterns of thought and action in terms of whether or not they facilitate or contribute to that purpose.

The sun is massive, stays on its own course, and has a gravity of its own. The root of the word gravity means "weight" or "heavy." The Romans considered gravitas a virtue, particularly in leaders. Speaking with gravity means conveying that weight by showing that you take yourself seriously and that you are firm and will be "difficult to move" if you believe that your cause is righteous.

This does not mean that you will never compromise or change your mind over time— that would be foolish and unwise — but it does convey a certain integrity and trustworthiness. People who change their beliefs depending on who they are talking to eventually reveal themselves to be untrustworthy because their marks eventually compare notes.

ORDER

As things shoot and move and float around them, objects with mass and weight and gravity are creators of orders and systems. Each sun is a creator of cosmos, of order, in the midst of the greatest chaos, the expansive disorienting void of outer space.

Man seeks order and in the absence of order, creates his own provisional order. He does this with his environment, with the people around him, and his own psyche. Consciousness itself is cosmo-generative.

The creation of order is the primary characteristic of solarity.

Do not confuse defiant creation with defiance for the sake of defiance. Defiant creation defies disorder to create order or rejects stagnant orthodoxy to improve an existing order. Defiance for its own sake merely perpetuates chaos.

ILLUMINATION

Be a calm source of illumination that reveals truth, whether it is ugly or beautiful. Seek out the truth of things and share it with those who are interested or ready to hear it — but don't become another street corner prophet shouting at strangers.

Solarity is a paternal concept, so telling people the truth doesn't always mean telling people what they want to hear. Sometimes it means telling them an uncomfortable truth that they need to hear — without malice or anger.

Do not confuse the revelation of truth with petty, trashy, and malicious gossip. The prevailing Zeitgeist is salacious and gossip-driven. Anyone can be embarrassed and stripped of dignity. Few would want to be photographed on the toilet, though nothing is inherently wrong or shameful about going to the bathroom. What is the cumulative, overall truth of a person? What have they accomplished? How have they helped and inspired others? How do they treat the people around them?
Reveal the simple truth, like the sun at noon.

Human life is more beautiful and interesting with an interplay of light and shadow, and there is value in mystery, but do not rely on shadow to obscure and deceive. Beware of people who romanticize the dark and want to remain in the shadows. What truth are they hiding?

Be the light, and let the shadow reveal its absence.

WARMTH

Without the sun, the earth would be a frozen rock shooting through space.

Take a moment to think about how life-giving that makes the sun. Every forest and field and jungle and blade of grass on earth reaches toward it and depends on it. No animals, much less men, would be able to survive on earth without it.

The sun can be blinding, and you can die from overexposure to its light. It is not benign, but it is, for the most part, benevolent — if we anthropomorphize a bit.

Are you a source of life-giving warmth in the lives of the people around you, or a collapsed sun— a black hole that draws them in and crushes them? Do the people in your orbit and the people you come in contact with every day feel improved by your presence? Do you make the people around you better or worse?

People love to complain, but it doesn't help them. Be a source of inspiration, not commiseration.

The sun has warmth and energy to spare. What it gives doesn't deplete it in any meaningful way.

Don't operate in a "zero-sum" frame. Most of us are mobile, and we aren't fighting over some closed, tiny market of friends, potential partners, or potential clients. Adopting an abundance mentality makes you appear more confident and less desperate — and ideally, you will also become more confident and less desperate.

Let the low-energy vermin fight over every scrap in the alley, and turn your mind to greater concerns.

CONCLUSION

Any one of the virtues I've described above has been exalted by any number of religions, philosophies, and motivational books. None of them are new. Each can be expanded upon and developed substantially.

Men have idealized and modeled themselves after sky fathers and solar entities for thousands of years. The sun is a powerful symbol — in fact, I can't think of a symbol more figuratively or physically powerful. The sun is unifying and universal. We can all look upward to see and contemplate the same sun. We can look inward and cultivate our own solarity. There's nothing arcane about the sun, and nothing could be less "occult" — less hidden or secret.

The slogan "stay solar" seems to have resonated with a lot of men, even men who years ago would have considered themselves drawn to darker or more oppositional ideologies. I believe that's because it's the right message, and it is the message men need right now. We live in an age of unhinged hysteria, where people feel compelled to react to or comment on a relentless barrage of trending outrages and curated "news" about strangers. All the old rules are in flux, and no one seems to know what the new rules are yet.

So, when you are surrounded by all of this confusion and anger, be like the sun. Remember who you are and who you want to be. You're the man, so be the man. Be the order. Be the light. In the midst of chaos and darkness, stay solar.

It's a little like that line from Kipling's "If."

> *"If you can keep your head when all about you, are losing theirs and blaming it on you..."*

Cultivating solarity is a response to darkness and confusion and anger and anxiety. It is a response to cynical nihilism, but it requires no retreat into childish naiveté or delusion. It's optimistic, but not foolish. It's a positive response to negativity. And it's a personal response because it starts with you.

I do not claim to be the perfect embodiment of any of the virtues or ideas I have espoused above. I'm going to put the best of myself forward, but I believe that the world loves nothing more than to see the inevitable deflation of men who puff out their chests too far, claiming to be something that they are not. The gods have always punished hubris, and I value humility in myself and the men whom I admire. As I have written in the past, "this is for me, too." Writers who connect with men authentically write the things they themselves want to read or need to hear. These are virtues I'm working on myself, not just preaching to others.

Men can all do better, and we can all try a little harder to *be* and to *stay* solar.

CPSIA information can be obtained
at www.ICGtesting.com
Printed in the USA
BVHW071520260421
605863BV00006B/1160

9 780985 452384